YORKSHIRE'S MULTIPLE KILLERS

Yorkshire's Multiple Killers

1915-2006

CHARLES RICKELL

Wharncliffe Books

First Published in Great Britain in 2007 by
Wharncliffe Books
an imprint of
Pen and Sword Books Limited,
47 Church Street, Barnsley,
South Yorkshire. S70 2AS

ISBN: 978 1 84563 0 225

A CIP catalogue record of this book is available from the
British Library

Typeset in Plantin and Benguiat by
Pen and Sword Books Ltd

Printed in the United Kingdom by
CPI UK

Pen & Sword Books Ltd incorporates the imprints of
Pen & Sword Aviation, Pen & Sword Maritime,
Pen & Sword Military, Wharncliffe Local History, Pen & Sword Select,
Pen & Sword Military Classics and Leo Cooper.

For a complete list of Pen & Sword titles please contact:
PEN & SWORD BOOKS LIMITED
47 Church Street, Barnsley, South Yorkshire, S70 2AS, England.
E-mail: enquiries@pen-and-sword.co.uk
Website: www.pen-and-sword.co.uk

Contents

Introduction and Acknowledgements

Convicted killers seldom repeat their terrible offence. You are more likely to win the jackpot in the National Lottery than being murdered by a repeat killer. However, since 1965 about 120 persons convicted of murder or manslaughter have killed again: either whilst on release or in confinement.

This book deals, for the first time in a single volume, with twenty-three convicted killers with Yorkshire associations, covering almost a century of modern crime from 1915 to 2005. In the cases of William Birkitt, Robert Mawdsley and Anthony O'Rourke, they even killed on a third, separate occasion.

Many of these cases raise the fundamental question of why such individuals were freed from prison, a situation which must be so distressing for the relatives and friends of the victims.

The reporting of homicide cases varies greatly in the Press of the day. Some receive widespread national coverage, others are just covered locally, even barely reported. Certainly until the 1960s, newspaper copy on the inquest, committal proceedings and the actual murder trial were generally available, especially locally or regionally. However, I have found that murder in prison receives scant regional newspaper coverage, unless a local person is involved.

For the convenience of the reader, the cases have been combined under the name of the person who has committed the killings, in chronological order of the first offence. A short summary has also been provided at the start of each chapter.

I would like to thank my editor, Brian Elliott for his help and suggestions. Carl Lawson has kindly provided several sketches. My wife, Theresa and daughter Rebecca have also been helpful and understanding whilst the research and writing has been in progress. Thanks are also due to Matthew Spicer for research on my behalf in The National Archives (formerly the Public Record

Office). David Speight supplied the additional photographs.

I am grateful to the staff of the Local Studies sections of the following libraries: Accrington, Barnsley, Belfast, Bradford, Halifax, Huddersfield, Hull, Leeds, Middlesbrough, Newport (Isle of Wight), Preston, Scarborough and South Shields. Their help is much appreciated.

Finally, specific assistance is acknowledged from librarians Deirdre Buck (Sheffield), Deborah Scriven (Wakefield) and Sue Rigby (York), now retired.

Chapter 1

William Burkitt

Hull, 1915, 1925
& 1939

William Burkitt killed three of his lovers. A Hull fisherman, he was convicted of manslaughter for killing his female married lover in 1915, but released from prison in 1923. Within a year, he brutally killed his second partner. Both crimes took place when he was under the influence of drink. After a further period of incarceration Burkitt killed yet again, in 1939 and was, despite a subsequent appeal, locked up for the rest of his natural life.

1. Hull 1915

I have done Polly in

At quarter to nine on the evening of Saturday, 28 August 1915, William Burkitt went to his mother's house in Worcester Terrace, Gillett Street, Hull. He told her that he had 'done it'. She asked him what he had done and he replied: 'I have done Polly in.' She asked him why and he told her: 'She won't tantalize anyone else.' He then said to his mother: 'Come with me and I will show you.'

Mary Ann Burkitt then accompanied her son to Derwent Avenue, Hull where Polly lived. When they got there Burkitt took a key out of his pocket and opened the door. He lit the gas light and pointed to a corner of the living room. When his mother looked she saw Polly laying in a pool of blood. She left the house and then Burkitt left, locking the door again.

Shortly afterwards, Burkitt saw Polly's young daughter, Flora Tyler and asked where her brother George was. She said he was at the pictures so he told her to fetch him. Flora asked Burkitt where her mother was and he replied that he would tell her when she brought her brother.

Burkitt returned to his mother's house and spoke to his brother, Harold. He told him he had killed Polly and handed him a badly bent knife which had blood on it. He then took his belt off and gave it and a halfpenny to his brother as keepsakes. He then repeated: 'I have done Polly in,' to which his brother responded: 'Is it true?' Burkitt held out his hand and Harold saw blood on his wrist. He again left the house and Harold soon followed – when he heard a cry in the street. It had come from Flora Tyler. Burkitt had met her in the street and given her the key, saying that her mother was dead. He told her to find a policeman and tell him to take her home.

Flora found Police Constable Marshall who went with her to the house. There he found Polly dead. He alerted the police station and a murder inquiry was launched. Later that night, he arrested Burkitt in Dock Road, Hull. When he told Burkitt that he was arresting him on suspicion of murder the latter said: 'Let's be going.' On the way to the police station Burkitt said to PC Marshall: 'She has brought me down to this.'

William Burkitt, a twenty-nine-year-old fisherman, was charged with the murder of Polly Tyler (whose real first-name was Mary Jane), aged thirty-two. She had been separated from her husband for twelve years and had been living with a man named Harding, who was also a fisherman. When Harding was at sea Burkitt would live with her if he was ashore. Her husband also used to visit her.

A post-mortem found that Tyler had been stabbed three or four times. A wound in her neck had severed her jugular vein. It was that wound that had killed her.

The case was heard on Tuesday, 23 November 1915, at the North and East Riding Assizes held at York Castle. Justice Atkin was the trial judge. Mr H S Cautley MP, and Mr L H Stanger acted for the prosecution. Burkitt was defended by Mr Rowan Hamilton.

Mr Cautley outlined the events leading to Polly's death. Early in August 1915, Burkitt had been fishing on a Scarborough-based boat. By mid-August, he was back ashore and returned to stay with Polly, in Hull. They lived together on good terms until 26 August. On that day they had argued over a photograph – taken in Scarborough – showing Burkitt with his arm around another woman. Polly had grabbed the picture and tore it up. The row got worse and Burkitt had threaten to blind her or 'do for her'. Worried, she left the house that night and stopped with a woman friend. The row continued the next day but they still went to the pictures. On the Saturday, Burkitt had been drinking and went to Polly's. The argument flared again and Burkitt stabbed Polly.

Polly's sister, Kate Elizabeth Witty of Saltburn Street, Hull gave evidence relating to Polly's life and background. When asked by Mr Rowan Hamilton if she knew Burkitt she said that she did not, nor did she know that Polly knew him.

Elizabeth Houghton of Malborough Avenue, Westbourne Street, Hull, told the court that she had known Polly as 'Mrs Harding' and had known Burkitt for three years. She knew that he stopped with Polly when Mr Harding was at sea. On Thursday, 26 August, a woman in Scarborough was mentioned and Polly had taken a photograph out of Burkitt's pocket; and she asked who the woman was. Burkitt said that it was someone he knew in Scarborough. Polly had then started arguing, using strong language. She got up and hit Burkitt then told him to go back to the woman as he did not want her. He refused to go saying: 'You have got my money and I am going to stay.' She carried on the argument even though Burkitt had threatened to blind her if she kept on. As the row developed further he threatened to 'do for her' and the lodger when he returned. They had some drinks and the row flared up yet again. Polly said that she dare not stop in the house that night so she stayed with her (Elizabeth) that night. Polly returned home the next day and Elizabeth called at her home. In the evening, Polly asked Elizabeth if her daughter would accompany her to the

YORKSHIRE ASSIZES.

SORDID HULL CASE.

WOMAN KILLED WITH FISH KNIFE.

SENTENCE OF 12 YEARS' PENAL SERVITUDE.

JUDGE AND DANGEROUS LINE OF JUSTIFICATION.

The Yorkshire Assizes for the North and East Ridings of Yorkshire were continued at York Castle, yesterday, before Mr. Justice Atkin

MURDER CHARGE REDUCED TO MANSLAUGHTER.

William Birkitt (29) was indicted on a charge of the wilful murder of Mary Jane Tyler, at Hull, on August 28th.

Mr. H. S. Cautley, M.P., and Mr. L. H. Stanger appeared for the prosecution, and Mr. Rowan Hamilton defended the prisoner who pleaded not guilty.

Mr. Cautley, in opening the case, stated that the deceased woman was 32 years of age and had been separated from her husband about 12 years. During the greater part of that time she lived with a man named Harding who was a fisherman. Whilst Harding was at sea the prisoner, who was also a fisherman, was in the habit of living with her when he came home from sea, and the woman's husband also visited her. At the time of the tragedy she was living at 4, Derwent-avenue, Hull. Previous to August 28th the prisoner had been fishing from Scarborough, and about ten days before that date he went back to Hull to have lived on very friendly terms with her until about August 26th when a quarrel arose about some girl with whom the prisoner had been living or with whom he had had his photograph taken at Scarborough. He produced a photograph of the girl and the deceased seized it and tore it up. She seemed to have provoked him by the language she used. and he used some serious threats, threatening to "blind her" and "do for her.

Extract from the Yorkshire Herald, *Wednesday, 24 November 1915.* Yorkshire Herald chemist's as she wanted to get some ointment to deal with spots on her face that Burkitt had complained about. Burkitt went with them to the chemist's. When they returned they argued again but then they went to the pictures. On the Saturday, Burkitt went to Elizabeth's and asked her if Polly was there. She told him that she was at her own home with friends but she would go and tell Polly that Burkitt was at her home. When she told Polly that Burkitt was at her home Polly said she would not go to see him. Elizabeth returned home and told Burkitt and he said he would go to Polly's. That was the last that she saw of either of them.

Mr Rowan Hamilton cross-examined Elizabeth. She said that Burkitt gave money to Polly when he was in Hull and sent her some when he was away. Burkitt had a very excitable nature and it was him who first took the photo from his pocket and showed it to Polly. She had hit him but he had not struck her, it was Polly who started the row. When they had returned from the chemist's the next day it was Polly who started the row again, he had just laughed. She thought he had been drinking when he turned up at her home on the Saturday afternoon.

Elizabeth's daughter, Eliza confirmed the arguments that her mother had witnessed and said that the photo showed Burkitt with his arm around a woman. She replied to Mr Rowan Hamilton that Polly had started the arguments and he had appeared drunk on the Saturday afternoon.

Elizabeth Bilton, also of Malborough Avenue, stated that she was in Polly's house on the Saturday afternoon and they seemed to be on the best of terms.

Burkitt's mother confirmed the conversation she had had with him on the Saturday evening. She said that she saw something covered in in what seemed to be a black coat, in the far corner of Polly's living room.

Harold Burkitt stated that his brother had told him that he had 'done Polly in' and had then given him his belt and a halfpenny to keep.

PC Marshall told the jury that he had found Polly's body and had arrested Burkitt later that night. Burkitt had asked him twice if he had found her wedding ring that she had thrown at him. On 2

September he had searched the house and found the ring near to where he had found Polly's body. He showed the court the knife that Burkitt had given to Harold. It was badly bent and was used for cutting fish.

Dr Moir, who examined Polly's body on the Saturday night, informed the court that he was sure that her wounds were not self-inflicted.

Dr J W Mason, police-surgeon, gave evidence of his post-mortem findings. The fatal blow was a deep stab wound just above the right collar bone, having severed the jugular vein. Another stab to the right shoulder was probably the blow that bent the knife. The attack had probably been sudden, brief and violent. Dr Mason was the last prosecution witness.

Mr Rowan Hamilton said that he would not be calling Burkitt to give his version of the events of that fateful night. He then addressed the jury, saying it was a tragedy that a mother had had to give evidence against her own son. He described Polly as a woman unfaithful to many men, constant to none. His client was probably the only man who had really loved her. He could not deny that Burkitt had killed Polly but he said that the jury would have to consider the provocation that he had endured on the Saturday and the days preceding it. They would have to consider whether the attack was premeditated and if he had committed it when he was in a overwhelming frenzy that rendered him – for the moment – incapable of realising what he was doing. He had begged and implored Polly to stop tantalizing him about a woman he did not care for but she had continued to argue and nag him. He told the jury that they could not convict him of murder. In view of all the circumstances a manslaughter verdict would be justified.

Justice Atkin advised the jury about taking provocation into account. He said that only Burkitt knew what happened that night but he had not given evidence. It was for the Crown to prove their case. Polly was a very violent woman and Burkitt was drunk at the time. His drunkenness should be remembered in his favour but did not excuse the crime. He remarked that if nagging by wives was justification to reduce a charge from murder to manslaughter it would be a very dangerous thing, and it was not the law.

The jury took just one hour to reach a verdict of manslaughter. Justice Atkin told Burkitt there could be no provocation sufficient to stab Polly. He had been at imminent risk of being convicted of murder. Burkitt was sentenced to twelve years imprisonment.

Burkitt's previous convictions included a bastardy case in November 1913. The following month he was convicted for arrears in relation to the same case. In November 1914, he had deserted from HMS *Hero* and in March 1915 he had deserted from HM trawler *Dinas*. In June he had been convicted of a breach of the peace. In the the Hull City Police records he is described as a stoker, five foot five and a half inches tall, with brown eyes, dark hair and complexion of medium build.

2. Hull 1925

He was very fond of her

William Burkitt was released from prison on 16 November 1924, having served nine of the twelve year sentence he was given for manslaughter. Within a year he was to kill again. His next victim was similar to his first.

Ellen Spencer, aged about forty-four, lived at Leslie's Avenue, Hull. She was separated from her husband Samuel and lived with a man called Sarginson. She also went out with William Burkitt and had been seen in the company of Sarginson whilst she was with Burkitt. The trio appeared to get on fine.

On Tuesday 3 November 1925, Mrs Matilda Walkington of Arthur's Grove, Manchester Street, Hull, Ellen's daughter, called at her mother's home but could not get an answer to her knocking. The front door was locked and the blinds were down. She went round to the back but found that the yard door was locked, so she climbed over the wall. Trying the back door, she found that it was also locked. She went to a neighbour of her mother, George Hamilton and asked for his help. He went with her to the back door and forced it open. They then went through the scullery and in the living room where they found Ellen on the couch, two overcoats covering her. Noticing blood on her mother's arms, Matilda removed the them and realised that she was dead. Leaving George with her mother's body, she went in search of a policeman. She found Police Constable Douthwaite and they returned to the house.

When PC Douthwaite entered the building he noticed a smell of gas so he quickly checked the ground floor to find the source of the leak. There was no sign of any emission so he went upstairs and found the source of the gas there. In the front bedroom the gas tap was open and a man lay on the bed. Turning it off, PC Douthwaite then went over to the man and found that he was unconscious, so started to apply artificial respiration. Dr Crawford, who had been alerted to the incident, arrived at the house and pronounced Ellen dead. He then went upstairs to help PC Douthwaite revive the man. William Burkitt, as he had now been identified, was put into an ambulance accompanied by PC Douthwaite. On the way to the hospital Burkitt regained consciousness and spoke to PC Douthwaite. According to the policeman, Burkitt said that he had stabbed 'her' on Monday night. When asked who he had stabbed he replied: 'The woman on the couch.' He also claimed that he was jealous of another man. Later on, PC Douthwaite's notes were read to Burkitt in the presence of a doctor; he was cautioned, then he agreed with the statement which said that he had used a pocket knife to kill Ellen and it was in the kitchen drawer.

Police Inspector Austin went to the house to examine the scene. During his search of the building he found the pocket knife in the kitchen drawer. There did not appear to be any blood on it. However, subsequent analysis found blood in the nick on the blade. A hammer with blood on its shaft was also discovered but it had not been used in the attack on Ellen. Inspector Austin also found Burkitt's trousers, waistcoat and boots in the kitchen. There

MOTHER'S BODY ON A COUCH.

TRAGEDY IN A HULL HOUSE.

FISHERMAN ON TRIAL AT YORK

Before Mr. Justice Fraser at the Yorkshire Assizes at York Castle, to-day, the trial took place of William Burkitt (40) a fisherman, of Hull, between November 2 and 3. Prisoner was further indicted with having attempted to commit suicide.

Mr. Donald Ross was counsel for the prosecution, and Mr. R. F. Burnand defended Burkitt. Four women were empanelled on the jury Burkitt pleaded not guilty.

VERY FRIENDLY.

Mr. Donald Ross said the deceased woman was about 44 years old, and she was the wife of Samuel Spencer, from whom she had been separated for some time. She had lived with a man called Sarginson, whose employment took him to sea. There was evidence that she knew prisoner, and they used to go about together, in fact, on the Sunday before the crime, she had spent most of the day in her mother's house, Burkitt being there for some time. So far as one could see they were on very friendly terms, and they had been seen out there being any appearance of any quarrel between them at all.

Extract from the Yorkshire Evening Press, *Friday 20 November 1925.* Yorkshire Evening Press was a spot of blood on one of the boots. There appeared to have been blood on the knees of his trousers but attempts had been made to remove it. He could not find any signs of a struggle having occurred in the living room. Following further inquiries Burkitt was charged with murder.

Burkitt's second murder trial was held on Friday, 20 November 1925 at York Castle with Justice Fraser presiding. The jury consisted of eight men and four women. Mr Donald Ross was the prosecution counsel. He outlined the case and then called witnesses to support it.

Henry Coley, Ellen's brother, said that she had lived with Sarginson, who was a ship's cook, for fourteen years. Cross-examined by Burkitt's counsel, Mr R F Burnand, he said that Ellen and Burkitt were on 'perfectly good terms'. Burkitt had a drink or two on the Sunday but was not inebriated. On the Monday he had not been drinking heavily. He did not know when Burkitt had returned from sea and he did not think that he drank a lot.

The next witness was Gertrude Lawrence of Leslie's Avenue. At eleven o'clock on the Monday morning she had seen Ellen going to a shop opposite the terrace where they lived. She knew Burkitt by sight but had never spoken to him. She had seen him on the Monday, in the street with two other fishermen, walking from the docks. She had on earlier occasions seen him with Ellen and had seen him enter Ellen's home. She had gone to bed at nine o'clock on Monday night and had not heard any unusual sounds coming from Ellen's house.

Ellen's daughter, Matilda told the court that after the back door had been forced she had found her mother with two coats covering her head. One of the coats was her mother's the other was a man's coat. The last time she had seen her mother was a fortnight before her death.

PC Douthwaite said that Burkitt's statement made in the ambulance was a perfectly voluntary one. Questioned by Mr Burnand, he admitted that he did not know whose knife it was as he had not made any enquiries about it. He had not considered Burkitt was too ill to talk in the ambulance, as he thought that he knew what he was saying at the time.

Dr Corbett identified the cause of death as a puncture wound about quarter of an inch long but deeper, which had cut the jugular vein. There were a few more puncture wounds but these had not been fatal. He said that the wounds could have been caused by the pocket knife found in the kitchen drawer. He had seen Burkitt in the hospital, and by then he had almost recovered from the effects of coal gas poisoning. Dr Corbett had plenty of experience of cases of coal-gas poisoning. Mr Donald Ross, prosecuting, asked him if he thought that Burkitt had been badly or lightly gassed. Dr Corbett replied that he was certainly not badly gassed when he saw Burkitt. Asked about Burkitt's mental condition at the time, he said Burkitt had asked him for a glass of cold water in a clear voice.

Inspector Austin gave evidence concerning his investigation. He had found the knife in a drawer. The knife was open when he found it. He had found a hammer in the scullery. The back door had been tied shut with string that had been threaded through a hook and secured to two nails. This could explain the blood found on the hammer handle. It was not used to attack Ellen but if Burkitt had blood on his hand it would have been transferred when he hammered in the nails. He had found a pair of boots in the living room and in the bedroom he had found a pair of trousers and a waistcoat. Burkitt had identified the items as his clothes. Later when he was questioned about his involvement in Ellen's death, Burkitt said: 'That is right.' Inspector Austin admitted that he had made no attempt to identify who owned the pocket knife.

The final prosecution witness was Arnold B Tankard, Hull City analyst, who gave evidence concerning the bloodstains which he said could be animal or human.

Burkitt was called to give his evidence. He said he was a thirty-nine-year-old trawler's fireman. He had first met Ellen several years ago. He had returned from sea on the 29 October and had seen Ellen on the Saturday morning. He had had a few beers at the *Half-way House* and the *Myton Tavern*, leaving the latter with a few bottles of beer. He had gone drinking the next day and had seen Ellen at eleven o'clock on the Monday. He told her about some new work he had got and she had gone to fetch some beer (this would have been when her neighbour had seen her). He had left at about noon and returned to his home. After that he had gone to the *Waffand Arms* in West Dock Street where he drank seven pints.

From there he went to Leslie's Avenue and laid down on the couch.

He stated that he was woken when he felt Ellen's hand in one of his pockets. He jumped up and threw her on the couch. Putting his hand on the table, he picked up something and held his hand up to frighten her. He then brought his hand down and then brought it down again. He then realised it was a knife he had been holding. He put the knife in the drawer and then covered Ellen with the coats. Asked by his counsel what effect the beer had had on him he replied: 'It had an effect on me.' He was also asked if he had any intention of killing Ellen. 'No,' was the reply. Had he ever any intention of hurting her? 'No, none whatever,' he said.

He remembered turning the gas off and securing the back door before he went upstairs. The next person he had seen was PC Dunthwaite. He only remembered making one statement that he had stabbed her on the couch. He was not in the habit of taking large quanties of drink.

Mr Donald Ross then started his cross-examination. Burkitt said that he was very fond of Ellen. When he had thrown her on the couch she had not resisted at all. He denied that he knew what he had picked up from the table. The crucial interchange between Ross and Burkitt went as follows:

Ross: 'What did you think you had picked up? Did you not think at all?'

Burkitt : 'No.'

Ross: 'You picked something up, as you say, absolutely reckless as to what it was ?'

Burkitt: 'Yes sir.'

Ross: 'Did you cut your hand?'

Burkitt: 'No.'

Ross: 'So you picked it up the right way by the handle, if you picked it up at all?'

Burkitt: 'Yes.'

Ross: 'And then you struck Ellen with it?'

Burkitt: 'I didn't intend to strike her.'

Ross: 'What did you intend to do?'

Burkitt: 'To frighten her.'

Ross: 'Do you seriously tell the jury that that when you inflicted those wounds on Ellen's neck you were merely trying to menace her and frighten her with the knife?'

Burkitt: 'That is right, sir.'

Ross: 'Could you not have frightened her with your fist?'

Burkitt: 'Yes.'

Ross: 'Do you remember the knife entering her neck?'

Burkitt: ' No.'

Ross: 'Your memory stopped short when you picked up the knife?'

Burkitt: 'Yes. When I saw the blood I realised that Ellen was hurt, then fastened the back door.

Ross: 'Why didn't you go out and get help?'

[No reply]

Ross: 'Did you not wish to save Ellen's life?'

[No reply]

Ross: 'You told us that you were very fond of her and you saw she was hurt. Did you not wish to try and get her some help?'

Burkitt: 'I saw her eyes open after I had hit her and I knew she was gone. She died practically instantaneously on being struck.'

Ross: 'Did you make any attempt to get any help at all?'

Burkitt: 'No.' (He said that he could not remember making any statement about being jealous, he was not jealous.)

Burkitt's counsel, addressing the jury, said that Burkitt's drunken state made a manslaughter verdict a more proper one than murder. The jury retired at two o'clock and during the luncheon interval they reached a verdict of manslaughter.

Inspector Austin was called to give Burkitt's record. The two desertions and his previous manslaughter conviction were reported. He had been released on a ticket of leave on the 23 November 1924. Since then he had served on five or six trawlers, being of good character. One trip had been for seven months in Icelandic waters. When ashore he was addicted to loose women and drink. He was born in 1887, the eldest of nine children. His mother was of good character.

Justice Fraser then passed a sentence of ten years – without making any other comment. It seems very odd that for a second offence of manslaughter he got two years less than he got for the first. His suicide attempt might have only occurred when he heard Matilda at the front door.

3. Hull 1939

I am fed up with her

William Burkitt, now aged fifty-three and a ship's fireman, returned home from the sea on 26 February 1939. He lived at Pleasant Place, Neptune Street, Hull, with Emma Brookes. Before he had set sail he had complained to his sister, Maria Kerslake, that Emma had been pawning his clothes and associating with other men. He had frequently complained to her about Emma's behaviour and even named two of the men. On 27 February, a young girl called at their home and saw them having dinner. She called again at about quarter to four and saw them again. As the girl left, a neighbour noticed that Burkitt locked the door behind her though that was not unusual. Emma was never seen alive again by anyone other than Birkitt. Shortly afterwards, another neighbour, Mrs Windsor, heard the sound of arguing coming from the house. It only lasted a few minutes and then she heard someone going up the stairs. She thought it was Emma. She had not heard anyone else go up the stairs and from then on the house was unusually quite. About an hour later, Burkitt was outside the house and he asked the young girl, who had called earlier,

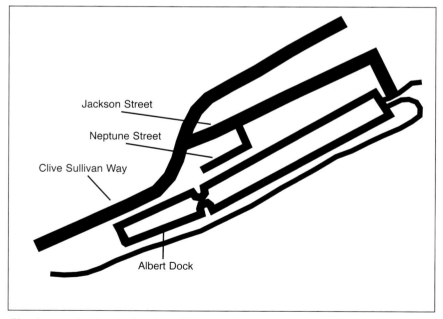

Sketch-map showing the location of Neptune Street. The Author

to go to the shop and get him some aspirins. At seven-fifteen that evening Birkitt was seen in an agitated state going along the street looking over his shoulder as he walked. He was not seen by anyone the following day.

At seven-forty on the morning of 1 March, Burkitt turned up at his sister's in Witty Street. He told her that he thought he was dying as he had taken 600 aspirin tablets. She had asked if Emma was all right. He replied: 'I don't know.' A little later, he said that he had caught her the previous day with another man. He left soon after and Maria followed him out, suggesting that he go see a doctor. He called back: 'No. Good bye. To tell you the truth I have killed her.' Maria lost sight of him as he went over Liverpool Street Bridge. Later that day, he was seen near a pile of timber, at Victoria Dock, in a dejected state. He was then seen struggling in the water and rescued from it by some men and taken to Hull Royal Infirmary.

Emma's body was found later that day. Inspector Davison had gone to 5 Pleasant Place following a tip-off. He broke in and found the downstairs rooms were in order. Going upstairs he found Emma's body on the bed, covered by bedclothes up to her waist. A jug containing a white liquid was found by the side of her. This liquid was later found to be water and aspirin.

Burkitt was wet and agitated upon admission at the Infirmary, when he was seen by Dr Henderson. He was arrested there on 4 March. As Detective Sergeant Barker went to caution him he turned away and said: 'I don't want to know, I am not going to listen.' DS Barker cautioned him and took him into custody on the charge of murdering Emma Brookes.

The case came to trial in Leeds before Justice Cassels on Wednesday, 17 May. Charles Paley Scott, KC, assisted by Mr G W Wrangham, prosecuted and Mr J Willoughby Jardine KC, assisted by Mr Alistair Sharp, represented Burkitt. There was a short interruption to the trial after the first witness gave evidence, as the whole air-raid warning system in Leeds was to be tested. Justice Cassels ordered a twenty-five minute adjournment and Burkitt was led below.

Mrs Emma Brookes and her husband had separated. Emma and Burkitt had lived at Pleasant Place since the previous June. Before that they had lodged in Hull with a Mrs Watkins. On one occasion during an argument Burkitt had his hands around Emma's throat. He said to Mrs Watkins: 'I will do for her.' When Mrs Watkins and her niece threatened to call the police he stopped choking Emma.

On another occasion he had said to Mrs Brookes' sister-in-law: 'Look at me I am in rags. Before many more weeks she will be a dead woman. She played with your brother for twenty-five years but she will not play with me. She will be a dead woman.' In February, Burkitt had told Mrs Watkins that he had caught Emma with a man and had threatened to 'do her in'.

Burkitt had gone back to sea in February and returned home on the 26th. The next day, Emma and Burkitt had been seen in a local public house and they appeared to be happy. Later that afternoon, Peggy Chester, aged fourteen, had gone to their home but she was told to come back later when Emma and Burkitt would take her to the pictures. She left their house at about three forty-five pm and shortly afterwards a neighbour, Mrs Florence Windsor, had heard the sound of an argument coming from the house. At four forty-five pm, another neighbour, Mrs Alice Rossington, saw a distraught and wild-looking Burkitt at the end of the terrace. He said: 'I am fed up with her. She is at it again.' Peggy returned at five forty-five pm and the door was locked, so she knocked. Burkitt opened the door and she asked if the 'missus' was ready for the pictures. Burkitt had replied: 'No, she does not feel very well, she is fast asleep.' When questioned, Peggy said that she thought it was funny that there was only a mug on the table because usually there would also be a cup. At seven-fifteen that evening, a woman who knew Burkitt saw him walking away from his home, and looking back over his shoulder as he walked away.

Mr Clarence Chester, licensee of the *Corporation Hotel*, Neptune Street, told the court that he knew the couple. Around Christmas, Burkitt had been downbeat and told him that he had found Emma in the company of some other men. He agreed that the couple seemed to be perfectly happy and that Burkitt was only a moderate drinker.

The divisional police surgeon, Dr M McLeod, stated that he had examined Emma's body. He found a small bruise on her left forehead which he thought was caused before her death. A man's fist could have caused the bruise, the blow could have been sufficient to stun a woman. There were bruises to both sides of her neck and a bone in her neck had been broken. The cause of death was asphyxia, from pressure applied to the throat. Justice Cassels asked if there was any signs of the woman struggling, but he found no evidence of this.

Burkitt went into the dock to give his version of events. He said they had been living together for two years and had always been happy together. He had cut her weekly allowance from 40s (£2) to 30s (£1.50) after she had started pawning his clothes. Around Christmas, he had found her associating with other men. On 27 February they had been drinking in a pub and Emma had asked him to buy her some beads and a purse. They had then gone to another pub and then to a jeweller's. He had given her half a crown (12.5p) for the beads but she still wanted the purse. They had tried all along Hessle Road but could not find a suitable one. They then returned to the *Chesters* pub and stayed about an hour, returning home at about three-thirty in the afternoon. When they got home, Emma said that she was going to bed and he had followed her upstairs. She had then mentioned the name of two men to him. Burkitt claimed that this came as such a shock, as he had been so good to her and had forgiven her, that everything 'went black'. Burkitt claimed that when he 'came round' he had his hand around Emma's throat, he could not believe it and called her name, then he kissed and shook her. He had then gone downstairs and when Peggy called he had asked her to get him aspirin. Later, he brought five more bottles of aspirin from different shops and mixed them into a paste. He took about three teaspoons of the mixture and was sick. The next he could remember was being on the dockside on the Wednesday. When cross-examined by Mr C Paley Scott, Burkitt denied he had made previous threats to Emma and that they had argued that afternoon. He also denied that Peggy had been in the house that day, claiming that when he met her at the top of the street she had asked him about going to the pictures. When it was suggested that he had crept up on her whilst she was asleep and then strangled her Burkitt said: 'No, she was awake'.

The jury returned a manslaughter verdict on Burkitt and he was sentenced to life imprisonment for his natural life. Justice Cassels commented that the jury had taken a merciful view.

In 1948, the *News of the World* carried a report that Burkitt had appealed against his natural life sentence. In the report it said that Burkitt was known in Hull as 'Fishy' or 'The Iron Man'. He had read debates in the House of Lords on the Criminal Justice Bill. His appeal was turned down by the Appeal Court. The Lord Chief Justice, Lord Goddard said that there was nothing in his contention that he had been sentenced to a term that was illegal, concluding that it was the only possible sentence.

In his application Burkitt had said: 'For nearly past ten years I have lived a living death in as much as that I have had held over my head the most dreadful sentence that has ever been uttered by a sane judge.' Burkitt appears to have forgotten that he was given a natural life sentence because he had killed on three separate occasions but a few lines later he then says: 'I would respectfully suggest that my past record should not have been held against me (either by the aforesaid judge or now during this inquiry) as I have paid for the past and paid in full.'

In Burkitt's file in The National Archives (formerly the Public Record Office) there is an undated cutting from the *News of the World*. It said that his sister, Mrs Maria Karslake, aged sixty-five, was asking for a police guard. Burkitt had been transferred from prison to a hospital in Hull, as he had an incurable illness. Two months earlier he had left the hospital but had been returned by the police four hours later. A Home Office spokesman said that if Burkitt committed another offence he would be returned to prison. He also said: 'You can take it for granted that the Home Secretary knew what he was doing. It is rare for a man to be kept in prison indefinitely.' Mrs Karslake did not get her police protection.

Chapter 2

Annie Neath

Bradford, 1917
and Halifax 1921

It was not unusual for single girls and young women living in service to become pregnant. The social stigma and fear of loss of employment following an 'unexpected' birth could result in great distress for the young mother – and criminal acts did occur. Annie Neath, a domestic servant, was charged and found guilty of killing her baby in 1918. She was subsequently imprisoned for manslaughter.

1. Bradford, 1917
She thought that it was dead

A wartime case that had very little coverage was that concerning Annie Neath. On Tuesday, 27 November 1917, the *Bradford Daily Argus* carried a small report on the inquest of a new-born baby found under a bed. Sarah Ann Myers worked at the *Junction Inn*, Leeds Road, Bradford as a domestic servant. On the morning of Sunday, 25 November her servant colleague, Annie Neath (Neate was the name given in the report) said that she was not feeling well. A doctor was called and Annie told him that she had given birth and wrapped the baby in two aprons before putting it under the bed. Sarah Myers told the inquest that Annie Neath had worked at the *Junction Inn* as a domestic since June and she understood that Annie was single. The report gave no indication as to the cause of death nor was it stated that Annie had been charged with any offence. It did say that the inquest was adjourned until 12 December. There was no report of the reopened inquest around that date.

The Junction Inn, *Leeds Road, Thornton, Bradford.* The Author

A small item appeared in the *Yorkshire Evening Post* on Friday, 15 March 1918. It said that at Leeds Assizes that day, Annie Elizabeth Neath, a twenty-four-year-old servant of Bradford, had been charged with the murder of her new-born baby in Bradford on 25 November. It was claimed that she stabbed the baby several times with scissors. Annie's defence was that the baby was premature and she thought it was dead; and that the injuries to the body were caused accidentally.

Child Under the Bed.

An inquest was held at the Town Hall to-day before the Bradford City Coroner (Mr. J. G. Hutchinson), concerning the death of a female child.

Sarah Ann Myers, a domestic servant, employed at the Junction Inn, Leeds Road, Bradford, said that Annie Neate, went as a domestic servant to the hotel last June. She gave the witness to understand that she was single. Last Sunday morning it was found that Neate had been confined. A doctor was sent for, and Neate informed him that she had had a child, and that she wrapped it in two aprons and placed it under the bed.

The inquest was adjourned until December 12.

She was acquitted on the murder charge but convicted of manslaughter. For this she was sentenced to eighteen months imprisonment without hard labour.

Typical press item relating to the Neate case. The Author

[On Monday 18 March 1918, the *Halifax Daily Guardian* carried a report on a similar case at Leeds Assizes. On Saturday, 16 March Sarah Ann Woodhead, a soldier's wife from Wibsey near Bradford was convicted of the manslaughter of her new-born baby. She had thrown it on a fire. Woodhead was sentenced to fifteen months.]

2. Halifax, 1921

He had his suspicions

George Hinchliffe and his wife Elizabeth lived at Rhodesia Avenue, Dryclough Lane, Halifax and employed Annie Neath as a general servant. She had worked for them since October 1919 but whether they knew of her previous manslaughter conviction is not known. On the morning of Saturday, 22 January 1921, Annie was fifteen minutes late in taking hot water to Elizabeth's room. When she saw Elizabeth at quarter to eight she asked if she could return to her bed as she did not fell well, she felt dizzy and had trouble standing. Elizabeth had asked Annie on Tuesday if she was all right because she had looked ill. Annie had said she was fine. That Saturday morning, Elizabeth told Annie to go to bed and called in to see her a little later. When she went into Annie's room she found her at her bedside but not in her bed so she told her to get into it. Elizabeth then noticed staining on the carpet near the bed. She asked Annie about the stain and Annie said that she had vomited. Elizabeth told her that it was a bloodstain and Annie replied that she had vomited up blood.

Elizabeth phoned Dr Roderick John Mackay and he was soon at

Rhodesia Avenue, Halifax. The Author

the house. He saw that Annie was very pale and asked about her condition. She told him she had been taken bad during the night, had vomited blood and had severe pains in her inside. Dr Mackay questioned her to see if she had either had a miscarriage or given birth – but she denied either situation. She said that a few months before some boys had knocked her down in the street and it had

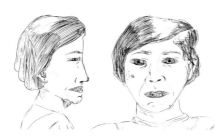

Sketch of Anne Neate. Carl Lawson

caused a lump. Dr Mackay said he would call back in the afternoon to see how Annie was getting on. At half-past four he returned and saw her again. Annie's condition was the same so he said he would call the next day. At half-past eleven on the Sunday morning he saw her again. As she appeared to have

improved, he gave her a more detailed examination. He told Elizabeth that a nurse should keep an eye on Annie. Elizabeth then contacted Martha Metcalfe of Huddersfield Road. Whilst changing Annie's clothing she noticed that her body was abnormal so she asked Annie about it. Annie said that she had fallen as a child.

On the Monday, Dr Mackay called again and, following another examination, told Annie that she needed to go to hospital for an operation. Annie gave her consent. As she had been due to return home to tend her ill mother, she asked Elizabeth to contact her and tell her she would be a few days. At eleven that morning an ambulance took Annie and Elizabeth to the Halifax Infirmary. Before leaving, Elizabeth told her that as she had a replacement servant coming she would need her room, she then asked if she could do anything for her. Annie asked Elizabeth if she would pack her things for her so she could pick them up when she left hospital. She told Elizabeth that her wicker dress basket was under the bed, there were some things in it and would she put them on top of it.

Dr W E H Banks, a house surgeon at the Infirmary conducted an operation on Annie whilst she was under anaesthetic. Whilst this was going on a gruesome discovery was made in Rhodesia Avenue. Elizabeth had arrived home at twenty-past twelve that afternoon and found a friend waiting for her. Before settling down to talk to her friend she went to Annie's room to make sure the window was open and tidy it up for the new servant. She was going to sort Annie's things out after her friend had left. She decided to pull the basket from under the bed but, removing the lid, saw a bundle with clothing on top of it. The sight of the bundle made her frightened so she went downstairs to her friend and asked her to accompany her to the room. With her friend beside her, she removed the bundle of clothing and saw the face of a new-born baby. Elizabeth then contacted her husband who rang Dr Mackay.

Dr Mackay arrived at the house at half-past five that afternoon and looked in the basket. Looking into the bundle, he saw a male new-born baby with blood on it. He noticed various bloody areas, one on the head the rest around the chest, he also thought that there were scratches on the body. Dr Mackay then told the Hinchliffes that the police would need to be informed.

At twenty to six, Chief Inspector Sykes and Detective Sergeant Matthews, of the Halifax Police, arrived at the house. Looking at the body they knew that they had a suspicious death to investigate. They carried out a search and found a pair of bloodstained scissors between the cotton cover and wire mattress. In the kitchen, a drawer used by Annie was found to contain a book called *The Midwife's Pronouncing Dictionary*. Two of the pages had been folded back. The baby's body was then removed to the mortuary.

The next day, Dr Mackay conducted a post-mortem on the baby. The fully developed male baby weighed seven pounds one ounce and it had been born recently. There were thirteen wounds on the body, twelve, three-eighths of an inch wide, appeared to be caused by the same weapon. Five of the wounds were in the area of the heart and one of the wounds had pierced it – this would have been fatal. Two pierced the brain, another in the throat had gone to the vertebrae, whilst the remaining ones had punctured the lungs and liver. Most of the wounds contained effused blood and had been inflicted before death. There was also a bruise behind the right ear.

On Tuesday, 25 January, Mr E W Norris the local coroner, opened an inquest into the new born baby's death. After hearing from Elizabeth Hinchliffe and Detective Sergeant Matthews he adjourned the inquest until Wednesday 16 February when it would be reconvened before an eight-person jury.

The police kept in contact with the hospital and were waiting when Annie Neath was discharged on Tuesday, 8 February. Detective Sergeant Matthews took her by ambulance to Halifax Police station where she was cautioned and charged her with the murder of her baby.

On 16 February, the inquest jury heard evidence from Elizabeth Hinchliffe, Detective Sergeant Matthews, Dr Mackay, Martha Metcalfe and Dr W E H Banks. Mr Norris then told the jury that they would have to decide that the child had lived. If the jury thought that it had they would have to decide if its death was due to the puncture wounds. If they were satisfied that the child had died from these injuries, they would need to consider who was perpetrator. He told the jury that if they decided that Annie had killed the child then a wilful murder charge should be returned against her. It would at a subsequent trial that the state of her mind at the time would be considered. Mr J H Mackrell, representing Annie, told the coroner that his client had no desire to give evidence. Mr Norris then read over all of the evidence to the jury. A juryman then asked Dr Mackay if a woman would have the strength shortly after giving birth, to inflict the stab wounds he had described. Dr Mackay replied: 'Oh, yes, quite.'

The jury retired for ten minutes and then returned with its verdict. It was decided that Annie Neath was the mother of the child, that the child had a separate existence and died due to the wounds inflicted by her.

Mr Norris said that this was the equivalent to a verdict of murder and committed her for trial at the next assizes at Leeds.

The next day, at the Halifax Borough Court, she appeared before the magistrates, having been remanded on two previous occasions. They knew of the inquest verdict and they heard some evidence. The Chairman of the Bench said they had no option but to commit her to the next assizes on the murder charge. Mr Mackrell asked the Bench to provide her with a certificate so she could pay for her defence at the assizes. This request was granted.

The trial of Annie Neath took place on Thursday, 17 March 1921 before Commissioner H J Young KC. Mr A E Capon prosecuted the case and Mr Willoughby Jardine defended Annie. There were three women on the jury. Mr Capon outlined the prosecution's case and then called Elizabeth Hinchliffe to give her evidence. She had barely started to give it when one of the jurymen complained that he was ill. After a ten minute adjournment, he was discharged and another person selected to replace him. The evidence was the same that had been heard at the inquest and committal proceedings. At a quarter to four the jury retired to consider their verdict. They returned an hour and a half later with their verdict: Annie Neath was guilty of wilful murder. They added a strong recommendation for mercy (even if they had known of her previous conviction for manslaughter they might still have recommended mercy). Commissioner Young did not put on the black cap as he sentenced her to death. She was reprieved and released on 22 May 1929. Annie had contacted tuberculosis whilst in prison and died from it in 1932.

Much earlier, in October 1900, another Halifax domestic servant had been on trial for killing her new born child in Heath Crescent, about two hundred yards from Rhodesia Avenue. The baby had been found in an outbuilding and the post-mortem revealed that paper had been stuck in its throat. It would seem that the jury gave her the benefit of the doubt as they acquitted her.

Chapter 3

Anthony O'Rourke

Pickering, 1949 & 1951
Slough, 1962

In 1949, Anthony O'Rourke was perhaps fortunate to escape a murder or manslaughter charge following the death of his former landlord whom he had struck on the head with a poker during a fight. Two years later, O'Rourke was on trial again, for the murder of Rose Harper, his ex-landlady. This time, he was convicted of manslaughter and gaoled for ten years. On release bouts of crime continued, culminating in the murder of his new wife, Florence in 1962. Sentenced to life, this three-times killer died in prison in 1995.

1. Pickering, 1949

It was self defence

Francis Postill returned to his lodging in Willowgate, Pickering at four-thirty on the afternoon of Saturday, 5 November 1949. He tried the door but found it was locked, so he looked for the key in its usual hiding place but it was not there. He was annoyed with his landlord, Tom Pickering, for not leaving the key. He waited and waited until nine-thirty that evening when his neighbours became concerned about Tom's absence. One of them, a Mr Fenwick, tried the door. When he could not get in he listened at the door as the curtains were drawn. He heard groaning from inside so he broke a window to get in. He found Tom lying injured on the floor. He went to the door but there was no key in the lock so he forced it open. The police and a doctor were sent for and Tom was conveyed to hospital.

The police soon had a suspect. Anthony O'Rourke, a previous

lodger, had been seen in the street at twenty-to-one that afternoon. Later on, Mr Leng, who lived at 7 Willowgate, saw him coming from the direction of Tom's house. The police went to O'Rourke's latest abode in Castlegate. His girlfriend, Florrie Marshall, who had four children, said she did not know where he was.

On 7 November, an operation was performed to remove bone fragments from Tom's brain. About the same time the police discovered that a tobacco coupon with the name T H Pickering had been exchanged in Scarborough on the day of the attack. The next major development was when a postcard arrived for Florrie. It had a postmark from Stockton on Tees dated the 10th. In it O'Rourke asked her to meet him at eight-thirty that Friday night. The police started to look for him in Stockton but could not find him there.

He was found a few days later at his home in Castlegate. When questioned about the assault on Tom, he made a statement. He claimed that he was walking along Willowgate when Tom called him, saying he had a letter from O'Rourke's mother. Tom said that she had been complaining about Florrie. They had then argued and fought, during which he had struck Tom on the head with something but he could not remember what he used. He had little recollection of the incident and could not remember what he did with the key. O'Rourke was charged with intent to cause grievous bodily harm.

The police obtained a statement from Tom in the hospital. Even though his health was improving, they decided to get a deposition so, on 5 December, with O'Rourke and a magistrate at his bedside, he gave his statement. He said that he was sitting down when O'Rourke came in and also sat down. They were talking and he then recalled being hit on the head. He did not know how or with what he was hit. As the blood ran down his face he asked O'Rourke to open the door but he did not. He did not remember arguing with O'Rourke.

Tom's health did not improve and he died on Tuesday, 15 December 1949. A post-mortem revealed that his death was due to hypostatic pneumonia that had developed due to septic meningitis which had been caused by his head injuries; he also had a broken rib. As Tom's death was due to the injuries allegedly committed by

O'Rourke, the latter was charged with his murder.

The case should have been tried at York Assizes but as the case list was full it was transferred to Leeds. The prosecution case was presented by Ralph Cleworth KC and O'Rourke was defended by Ernest Ould (who later became a judge), assisted by John Parris. Just before the trial started, John Parris had a conference with O'Rourke. Parris explained that even if the jury accepted his version of the events they would still convict him of manslaughter. He told O'Rourke that a self-defence plea could only work if he had no opportunity to retreat. O'Rourke then came up with a slightly different version of the events.

Mr Cleworth described the case as the brutal murder of a defenceless old man struck on the head with a poker. He also said that O'Rourke had left the wounded old man and locked him in the house and failed to get him medical treatment. He also took tobacco coupons from the house.

Florence Marshall was called to give evidence for the prosecution. She was asked about O'Rourke's absence from their lodgings from 5-13 November. She also identified the letter that he had sent to her. Ernest Ould cross-examined her. She explained that whilst they had lodged with Pickering he had made immoral suggestions to her; she had been afraid of him and he had turned nasty when she had refused him. She had not told O'Rourke about his behaviour. In his book *Most Of My Murders*, O'Rourke's junior counsel, John Parris said that he thought it was a mistake for the prosecution to call Florence as a witness. He believed that her appearance in the witness stand and the answers she gave helped turn the victim from a pathetic old man with his head bashed in, into a dirty old man.

The defence tried to argue that Tom had died from the septic cystitis and silicosis that he was found to be suffering from when the post-mortem was carried out. They said the pneumonia could have been brought on by either of two pre-existing conditions. Justice Streatfeild clarified this point during his summing up. He told the jury that it was enough for the prosecution to show death had been hastened or aggravated by the blow.

O'Rourke chose to give evidence. He had no reason to argue

with Tom but on 5 November Tom had called him over, saying that he had received a letter from O'Rourke's mother. Tom said that in the letter she had said that Florence was 'no good'. Tom had then said he had been with Florence and had paid her. They had quarrelled and Tom had grabbed O'Rourke's pullover, during the struggle they fell across the fireplace fender with Tom on top. Tom had reached for a poker and was about to strike O'Rourke but he had snatched the poker off him and had struck Tom on the head with it. O'Rourke had added the point about being on the floor with Tom on top in response to John Parris' comment regarding the point about self-defence. O'Rourke could not retreat because he was underneath Tom. Even if O'Rorke's new version was true it did not explain why once he had disarmed Tom he had struck him, the threat to life had been removed when he gained possession of the poker. After all, O'Rourke was younger and a labourer whereas his victim was an elderly man. In Tom's hospital statement he said that they were both seated when he was attacked.

O'Rourke explained that he had taken the tobacco coupon by mistake. When leaving the house he had seen a piece of paper on the floor and thinking he had dropped it he had picked it up. That did not explain why he had then gone and used it on the same day.

During O'Rourke's cross-examination, the prosecution failed to ask why he had not mentioned the self-defence before, nor why he had drawn the curtains and locked the door. What money he lived on before he returned to his home, had he stolen money from Tom? How could he explain Tom's statement that they were both seated when he was struck? Why had Rourke not summoned medical aid after hitting an old man on the head?

In his summing up, Justice Streatfeild told the jury there were three possible verdicts: murder, manslaughter or not guilty. It took the jury two and a half hours to reach a conclusion. They acquitted him of murder and of manslaughter and O'Rourke left the dock and returned home. We do not know if the jury believed O'Rourke's story or if they thought Tom had died from his pre-existing illness.

2. Pickering, 1951

He returned to the scene

Sergeant Brown was on duty at Pickering police station at six-thirty on the morning of Tuesday, 5 June 1951 when Anthony O'Rourke entered and said: 'I killed Rose Harper yesterday.' Sergeant Brown's surprise was not as great as it could have been, since at ten o'clock the previous evening he had searched Rose's home by candlelight after her friends had expressed their concern to the police. At nine o'clock that evening they had called on her but her door was locked. This was unusual so they borrowed a ladder and climbed into the front bedroom. The room appeared ransacked so they searched the rest of the house and could not find her, that was when they went for the police.

Sergeant Brown returned to the house, as it was now daylight so he could see more clearly. This time he saw two bare feet protruding from under the living-room table. Moving a chair, he got under the table and removed a rug, and found Rose's body. A stocking was tied around her neck and a handkerchief was stuffed in her mouth. Anthony O'Rourke, an unemployed twenty-nine-year-old, was charged with the murder of Rose Hannah Harper, a fifty-five-year-old charwoman at her home at Westgate, Pickering on 4 June 1951.

The case came to trial at Leeds. Justice Pearson presided, Harold Shepherd KC, prosecuted and John Parris defended O'Rourke. The prosecution case was that O'Rourke had attacked Rose, who was a friend and former landlady, to steal items from her home. At one, early on the Tuesday morning, O'Rourke had returned to her home (after Sergeant Brown had been to look for Rose at her home and O'Rourke turning up at the Police Station) in a taxi and removed several items including a radio, sewing machine and bedding. The taxi-driver was not suspicious because O'Rourke had told him it was his mother's house and he had a key to the front door. He then told the taxi driver to drive him to Castlegate, Pickering, and had given the taxi driver her watch and chain as he had no money to pay for his fare from Scarborough. It was claimed that he had caught the nine-thirty bus to Scarborough on the Monday morning, having first killed Rose shortly after eight. She

Westgate, Pickering. The Author

had returned a teapot to her neighbour just before eight am; and at seven-thirty O'Rourke was seen walking towards Westgate. At about quater-past eight he was seen walking towards his home. She had been manually strangled, the stocking had been applied later.

O'Rourke's defence was that he had previously given Rose £16 for the goods and merely took them because they were now his. He claimed that on the Monday morning he had gone to collect the goods at her invitation. She said that the sewing machine was in the bedroom and when they went up for it she had pushed him onto the bed. He had a cigarette in his mouth and the push made him burn his lip and he alleged that Rose suggested they have sex. He ran from the room and went downstairs. Rose had come down and made him a cup of tea and had then started suggesting that O'Rourke's common-law wife Florrie was a whore (similar to what he alleges happened at his previous trial). He claimed that he accidentally strangled her when she grabbed him by his private parts after he had called her a dirty old whore. He had stuffed the handkerchief in her mouth in case she had come to and started screaming. He had left the house and locked the door, after walking round for a while he returned and saw that she was dead. He then looked to see if any of the £16 he had paid her was in the house but could not find it. He left, locking the door once again. He then went to Scarborough and spent the day drinking. He decided that since he could not get his £16 back he would take the goods he had paid for. A prison doctor said that O'Rourke told him he had burnt his lip on the Sunday which cast doubt on his claim that it was burnt when Rose pushed him onto the bed. O'Rourke admitted that he had said that it happened on the Sunday but claimed he had not wanted to mention Rose pushing him onto the bed, his own counsel had not heard about it until he had told the court.

The jury convicted O'Rourke of manslaughter and he was sentenced to ten years' imprisonment. After the sentencing his counsel asked him asked him what really happened. He said that Rose had called him a murderer and he had lost his temper. His counsel had been worried that the prosecution might bring up the missing shoes. Rose was barefooted when she was found and no shoes had been found in the house. If the prosecution had accused him of stealing them (Rose would not have sold her only pair of shoes) the outcome could have been different.

3. Slough, 1962

She's gone to visit a nun

Having earned full remission for his manslaughter conviction of Rose Hannah Harper, Anothony O'Rourke was released from prison in 1958 and went to Walworth, London to join Florrie and his four step children. Whilst in prison his wife had divorced him and he had married Florrie (Florence Marshall), changed his own name to Regan. It wasn't long before he was on probation for stealing from a gas meter. The family then moved to a new estate at Britwell on the outskirts of Slough, Buckinghamshire. After a while, O'Rourke came to the attention of the local police. He had stolen some wage packets and was sent to prison for a year. He returned to the family home in

Long Reading Lane after his release from that sentence.

There was soon discord in the house. O'Rourke started to take an interest in his eldest step-daughter but this was not reciprocated. Florrie noticed that O'Rourke's interest in her was cooling whilst his unwanted attention on her eldest daughter was growing. They started to argue more often, the lack of money in the house added to the reasons to argue. When they argued O'Rourke, in an attempt to divert Florrie's accusations of his interest in her eldest daughter, would accuse Florrie of having an affair with a man called Solly whilst she lived in London.

Things came to ahead on Saturday 24 March 1962. They were out shopping when another row started. O'Rourke left Florrie in the town with their shopping and returned home alone; the house was empty as the step-children were out. When Florrie returned the row continued. O'Rourke was to claim later that she had said she was going to London for a drink with Solly. She had ignored him when he told her she could not go to meet Solly. Maybe Florrie had gone to their bedroom to get her coat but she was never to leave that room alive.

When the step children returned he told them that their mother had gone to stay with a nun in London. Florrie's eldest daughter rang the nun who told her that she had not spoken to her mother for six months. When she challenged O'Rourke about it he then said her mother had gone to stay with relatives in the North East. Even though she worked as a clerk in Slough, the eldest daughter was willing to help look after her brother and sisters. She did not stop in the family home long because O'Rourke told her that he loved her and later tried to rape her. O'Rourke explained to neighbours that his wife was taking a long holiday.

The long period without contact from her mother worried the eldest daughter. Three months after last seeing her mother she decided that she would have a look in her parent's bedroom, which had been kept locked since her mother left, when O'Rourke was out of the house. On Saturday 23 June she went to a neighbour's so that she could see when O'Rourke left the house. Once she had seen him leave she used the spare key that the neighbour had to gain entry. She managed to get into the bedroom and found a pile of her mother's clothes on the bed. She then realised that if her mother had gone to visit relatives she would have taken some of her clothes but they were still in the house. Leaving the family home she went to the police.

With O'Rourke's record and a report from a worried daughter that her mother was missing the police immediately took the matter seriously. Detective Inspector Henry Kennan and Inspector Aubrey Smith decided to visit the house, when they got there he was not there but they gained entry and made for the bedroom. On entering it they noticed a strong smell, an odour that O'Rorke had explained to the children came from a nearby farm. They started to lift the clothes from the bed, and as they removed them they came across Florrie's decomposed body. They continued their enquiries at the house whilst they awaited O'Rourke's return.

When he turned up at the family home later that day O'Rourke was charged with Florrie's murder. He made a statement in which he claimed that he had heard that Florrie had had an affair with Solly and on Saturday, 23 March they had argued in their bedroom; she had picked up the knife and attacked him. During the strugle he had stabbed her in the chest, but had applied a dressing to the wound and left the house. When he returned, Florrie was dead so he covered her body with clothes then locked the bedroom door to prevent her children seeing her corpse. O'Rourke appeared before Burnham magistrates charged with murder, and was remanded in custody. A post-mortem showed that Florrie had been stabbed in the chest twice.

On Tuesday, 17 July, O'Rourke appeared before the magistrates again. After hearing the outline of the prosecution case they committed O'Rourke for trial on a murder charge.

The trial was held at the Old Bailey in September 1962. Prosecuting counsel Mr Mervyn Griffiths-Jones QC told the court that Regan (O'Rourke) faced the murder charge and was also charged with the attempted murder and attempted rape of his oldest step-daughter. The prosecution case was that he murdered Florrie because of his lust for his eighteen-year-old step-daughter. A five-year diary had been found in the main bedroom. In the middle of the diary Regan had written: 'Dear Sir, I killed my wife on Saturday. I killed her with a knife in the chest. I loved my wife but I also loved my (step) daughter, aged 18. After killing my wife,

I put her in the wardrobe for a few weeks'.

The famous Home Office pathologist, Dr Francis Camps told the jury about his post-mortem examination of Florie's body. She had been stabbed twice, the wounds were about an inch apart. One of the wounds had punctured the main artery of the heart. He estimated that Florrie would have died within five minutes.

On the second day of the trial Regan's counsel, Mr Jeremy Hutchison QC called him to give his evidence. He asked Regan if he intended to cause his wife's death. Regan replied saying: 'No sir, I loved my wife.' In reply to a question about Florrie going to visit Solly, Regan gave his version of what happened. When he had told Florrie not to go to see Solly she was in a bad temper had picked up the kitchen knife that was in the drawer in the bedroom. She had attacked Regan who had grabbed her wrist to prevent her stabbing him. During the struggled Florrie had accidentally stabbed herself when they had fallen face first on the bed with him on top of her. He had turned her over and seen the blood on her chest.

Cross-examined by Mr Griffiths-Jones QC, Regan explained that he had not contacted the police when he had found out that Florrie was dead because he had panicked thinking they would accuse him of stabbing her. The jury were not aware that he had killed twice before so he could not explain to them why he thought it more than likely that the police would accuse him of Florrie's murder. Mr Griffiths-Jones pointed out that Regan's version of how Florrie came to be stabbed only accounted for one of the wounds. It was improbable that Florrie and fallen onto the knife then with Regan still on top of her, raised herself and fallen again onto the knife within an inch of the first wound. Instead of calling for an ambulance or the police he had hidden her body in the wardrobe. Regan had displayed his callousness by washing the knife that had killed the wife he claimed to love, and returned it to the kitchen.

In his closing arguments on behalf of Regan, Mr Hutchison QC, asked for a total acquittal if they felt that Florrie's death was accidental or a verdict of manslaughter if they thought Regan had not meant to seriously harm her. He claimed that if Regan had run to his neighbour, crying and pleading for help he would not be on trial. Instead, he panicked. This of course ignores the fact that with his record the police would not have believed his claim and he would have been charged.

On 19 September, the jury took three and a half hours to find him guilty of murder. Mr Justice Roskill told Regan that the jury, without knowing his previous convictions, had returned a just and true verdict. He then sentenced O'Rourke/Regan to natural life imprisonment. He ordered that the charges relating to his step-daughter remain on file in case a future Home Secretary considered releasing him. Under the 1957 Homicide Act it was a capital offence if someone previously convicted of murder was convicted of another murder that occurred at a later date. As O'Rourke/Regan's first conviction was for manslaughter the maximum penalty was life imprisonment. For Anthony O'Rourke it really was to be for his natural life. He died in prison, in March 1995.

Chapter 4

Donald Sheldon
Bradford, 1953 & 1976

Donald Sheldon fatally stabbed his former wife, Kathleen, in 1976, receiving a manslaughter verdict and a minimum sentence of fourteen years. Twenty-three years earlier, he had also been convicted of manslaughter, following the death of an infant girl. Due to terminal illness, he was unable to complete his final imprisonment, still maintaining that he loved Kathleen.

1. Bradford, 1953
The rattle in the pram brought it back to him

Donald Sheldon was a twenty-three-year-old unemployed warehouseman. He lived at Bishopdale Holme, Buttershaw, Bradford with his parents, girlfriend Sheila Collinson and their child Anne Collinson, aged seven months. On Friday, 18 December 1953, when the others went out for the night, he was left alone in the house with his daughter and his sister's baby. When the family returned later that night his younger brother found Anne dead in the bed. Sheldon had then left the house and walked to Bradford Police Station and spoke to Detective Constable Pilling. Sheldon told him that he had just killed his own daughter and then he broke down and wept. When he had regained his composure he said that Anne had woke up screaming, that he got hold of her but he could not remember what had happened then. He remembered being in the bedroom and finding Anne dead in the bed. Following further questioning, Sheldon was charged with murder.

A post-mortem showed that Anne had been seriously ill with enteritis and might have died within hours but Dr D E Price had

Bishopdale Holme, Buttershaw, Bradford. D Speight

found four slight bruises on the front and top of her head and there were mild signs of asphyxia. If he had not seen the slight bruises he would have been satisfied that death was because of toxemia, due to enteritis. In his view a pillow had been placed over Anne's face but not held there. The cause of death was toxemia accelerated by shock from head blows.

The inquest into Anne's death was held in Bradford on Monday, 18 January. Just before it opened Sheldon went up to Detective Constable Pilling and, before he entered the building, gave him two sheets of paper. He explained that after Christmas he had seen Anne's rattle lying among some clothes in a pram and he suddenly recalled what had happened that evening. He had written it down and that was what he had given to Detective Constable Pilling.

Sheldon's trial took place in Leeds on Monday, 1 March 1954 before Justice Pearson. The Crown's case was put by Geoffrey Veale, QC and A B Boyle. His defence was by J Stanley Snowden and Geoffrey Baker. Dr D E Price gave his findings concerning Anne's death. Mr Veale told the jury about the two-page letter that Sheldon had written. In the letter he had said that Anne was asleep in her pram, she woke up and started to cry and scream, her screaming had annoyed Sheldon so he had jumped up and put a pillow over her face until she died. He had then taken her from the pram and put her to bed, upstairs. Mr Veale said that a deliberate act that accelerated the death of a person was murder.

Sheldon's counsel argued that there was no case to answer as Anne was seriously ill but Justice Pearson rejected the submission. Sheldon gave evidence in his own defence, saying that he was very fond of Anne and had never struck her. He was unaware that her crying and screaming was because she was seriously ill. He had not thought to get assistance when he found her dead. The jury convicted him of manslaughter and Justice Pearson said he agreed with their verdict. He then sentenced Sheldon to three years 'corrective training' so that he could learn discipline and self-restraint. Sheldon had previous convictions for shop breaking, housebreaking and theft for which he had served borstal and prison sentences.

2. Bradford, 1976

He still loved her

Kathleen Sheldon, aged thirty-three, had been divorced from her forty-six-year-old husband, Donald for a year but she had recently moved in with him and his mistress at St Mary's Crescent, Wyke. They had five children but their marriage had had problems. In 1967, she had told him she had been unfaithful. His response had been to smash a beer glass in her face. She had seventeen stitches and a court ordered that Sheldon be treated in a mental hospital for a year. Donald Sheldon had been unemployed since heart trouble in 1971. Kathleen worked at a restaurant in Great Horton Road, Bradford.

On Saturday 7 August 1976, Donald Sheldon attacked her outside the restaurant where she was employed and stabbed her twice, fatally wounding her. On the following Monday, he appeared at court in Bradford, charged with murder.

An inquest was opened and adjourned by the coroner, James Turnbull, on the Wednesday. Detective Superintendent Dick

Holland told the inquest that Kathleen had suffered two stab wounds to the upper front part of her torso. The higher wound was near her breast bone and had cut her aorta, and had caused severe internal bleeding. The other wound had penetrated her diaphragm and liver. Miss Lorna Kirton, a lifelong friend, who lived with Mr and Mrs Sheldon, gave evidence of identification.

The case was tried at Leeds in December. Justice Boreham presided and Gerald Coles QC, prosecuted for the Crown. His defence team, led by Donald Herrod QC, tried to get a manslaughter verdict on the grounds of provocation. They had sought to use a diminished responsibility plea but a psychiatrist said he was not in that state at the time of the killing. The couple had divorced in 1975 but had continued living together. On Thursday, 16 December, the jury convicted Donald Sheldon of murder. Justice Boreham sentenced him to life with a recommendation that he serve at least fourteen years. It was then revealed that Sheldon had a previous conviction for manslaughter. Detective Sergeant Geoffrey Tottles said few details could be given as that offence had occurred more than twenty years ago and most of the records had been destroyed.

Sheldon did not serve the fourteen years that Justice Boreham specified. He was released after nearly ten years. On 20 November 1986, he was transferred from Kingston Prison, Portsmouth to a hospice in the town because he was dying from cancer. Whilst at the hospice, his son, John, and daughter-in-law, Marie, stayed with him for a week. He told John that he was sorry for what he had done and still loved Kathleen. He died, aged fifty-six, on 8 December 1986.

Chapter 5

Margaret Anne Wiggins

York, 1957
Malton, 1974

This very sad case relating to mental illness involves Margaret Wiggins, convicted twice for the drowning of her son and granddaughter over a seventeen-year period.

1. York, 1957

But I couldn't have done this

The parents of seven-year-old Colin Michael Wiggins called the police, at ten-thirty pm, on Tuesday, 26 November 1957, to report him missing. He had not returned to his home in Flaxman Avenue, York, after going to St George's Cinema that afternoon. Mr George Wiggins and his wife Margaret Anne had been looking for him since six-thirty the same evening. A search of the area was carried out. The Fire Brigade assisted with lighting equipment. Early the next morning the boy was spotted face down in the River Foss near Foss Island Road. It took a while to recover his body as it was in the middle of the river.

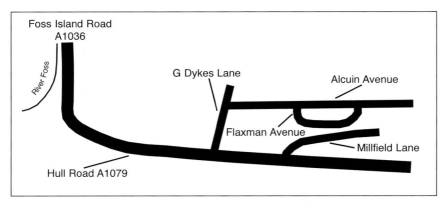

Sketch-map showing Flaxman Avenue and Foss Island Road. The Author

On Thursday, 28 November, the inquest into Colin Wiggins' death was opened at the York Law Courts. Mr Innes Ware, the coroner, took evidence of identification from Colin's father. He said to York's Chief Constable, Mr C Carter that he understood the post-mortem had been conducted and the cause of death was drowning. Mr Carter agreed but he had not yet received the full report. Mr Ware adjourned the inquest until 20 December. Colin was buried on 2 December.

On the evening of Thursday, 20 December, Margaret Anne Wiggins, aged forty, was taken to the police station. Detective Inspector J A Pickup cautioned her and charged her with her son, Colin's murder. She said: 'I couldn't have done, but I couldn't have done.' When Margaret appeared at the magistrates' court the next day, she was asked if she had anything to say as to why she should not be remanded in custody for a week. Her reply was: 'No sir, but I couldn't have done this.' She was granted legal aid and remanded in custody for a week. An outline of the case was heard on Thursday, 9 January when she was committed for trial at the next York Assizes.

The case came to trial on Monday, 17 February 1958 before Justice Finnemore. Margaret was defended by Mr P Stanley Price QC and Mr G Smailes. Mr G S Waller QC and Brian Boyle prosecuted the case. The procedings lasted five and a quarter hours. Mr Waller said that it was not their duty to prove any motive. Margaret lived in a council house with her husband and some of her children. She had four from a previous marriage; Colin and Roger were from the second marriage. On 26 November, Margaret Wiggins had been to the magistrates' clerks' office to see if there was any money for her with regard to a domestic matter. She had then gone to the cinema with Colin and Roger. She had returned home with Roger in his pushchair and asked her daughter, Margaret Ann Walmsley, aged nineteen, if Colin had come home from school.

At about ten-fifteen pm, William Roy Walmsley, her eighteen-year-old son from her previous marriage, arrived home to find her crying in the front room. He asked her why she was crying and his older brother Raymond said: 'Colin is drowned,' and his mother said: 'At the back of the Corporation.' He had gone to look but returned within ten minutes. Margaret then said that she had not meant to do it. She explained that she had 'tried to do herself in'. Colin had been at the side of the pushchair and the next minute he was gone. William said that his mother had always looked after her children very well, they had always been well-dressed and well-fed even though it had been a struggle at times. His mother had been in hospital on a number of occasions, the duration of the stays getting longer each time. By 1950, the stays could last a year and she would not be home for long before she returned to hospital. The last stay had lasted eighteen months. She was fond of Colin and her children but had tried to kill herself on previous occasions.

A cashier at St George's Cinema, Caroline Martin Lawson, said that a woman with a baby in her arms had brought tickets on that afternoon and if she had watched the entertainment when she would have left it would have been around six o'clock.

A plump woman with a child in a push chair and a young boy, wearing a maroon blazer, walking at her side, was seen near the entrance to an opening where the towpath branches away from the road. The last that Dennis George Armour saw of them was as the pushchair entered the opening. He said that he was not able to identify the woman.

Detective Harry Poller had asked Wiggins if it was probable she could have knocked or pushed Colin into the river. She had replied: 'Oh, I don't think so, I don't think that I would do that to Colly. I can't remember.' He said that there was a history of mental illness in her family, her father and two sisters having committed suicide.

Dr David Ernest Price, pathologist, said the cause of death was asphyxia due to drowning and the shock of immersion had probably contributed. There were no other injuries except for a few very slight marks on his face, which could have been caused as he struggled in the water. Colin appeared healthy, well nourished, clean and well looked after.

Sister-in-law, Alice Bellwood said that on the day of Colin's funeral Margaret had said she was going to give herself up. She had appeared very worried and upset as though she had something on her mind. She could not face going to his funeral but did go. Mrs Bellwood had offered to go with her if she went to the police but Margaret decided not to go. In reply to Mr Price, she said that Margaret did not seem to realize she had lost Colin, she also confirmed the mental problems within Margaret's family.

A consultant psychiatrist, Dr W Bowen, said that Margaret suffered from a reccurring form of mental illness characterised by a form of depression and epilepsy. In his opinion she was in this condition at the time of the offence and would not have known what she was doing nor that it was wrong. She had ideas of unworthiness and felt she had failed to look after her family. At times her mind went blank and she felt irresponsible. In reply to Mr Waller, he said that if she had pushed Colin in the river it would have been due to 'a disease of the mind'.

The Senior Medical Officer at Durham Prison, Dr J G W Pickering said that under care she had gradually returned to normal mental health.

Mr Price said that if the jury thought she had pushed Colin into the water then the correct verdict would be 'guilty but insane'. They had to decide if she was guilty at all, just because he had been found in the river it did not mean that she had murdered him.

Mr Waller's address to the jury referred to Margaret as 'an unfortunate creature'. Colin had been loved and well looked after by her but she had pushed him into the river so that he should be killed. He argued that she was either guilty or guilty but insane.

In his summing up, Justice Finnemore pointed out that it was stretching credulity a great deal to think that Colin had placed his cap near the wall before he fell into the river. The jury was dealing with a woman who, over a period of years, had suffered from serious mental health problems. She had epileptic attacks during which she could be aggressive, noisy and her mind would go blank. If Colin's death had occurred during one of these attacks she would not be criminally responsible.

The jury retired and were out for eighty-four minutes. Their verdict was 'guilty, but insane', and Justice Finnemore ordered that Margaret be detained at Her Majesty's Pleasure.

2. Malton, 1974

It must be in the river, musn't it?

It was the afternoon of Friday, 15 February 1974, when Margaret Ann Wiggins, a fifty-seven-year-old housewife of Ascot Way, Acomb, York decided to take her granddaughter to Scarborough. Her daughter, Mrs Diane Wade, lived in Middleton Road, Acomb, with her partner, John Roland Thomas and their daughter Melana Thomas, aged five months. Diane had left Melana at home with Margaret whilst she went out to do some shopping. It was the first time that Melana had been left alone with grandmother Margaret. When Diane returned at two pm, her mother, Melana and her pushchair where missing. Diane searched the local area until six pm when she informed the police.

The search proved fruitless and their fate only became apparent

Looking towards the bridge at Malton. The Author

The old bridge at Malton. The Author

at four o'clock the next afternoon when Margaret approached a woman police officer in Leeds and asked where there was a police station. She said to the officer that she had lost her little boy (not her grand daughter) and that he was in Scarborough. She said: 'They are looking for me. This is me'. She was pointing to a headline in a Leeds paper. Asked where the baby was, she replied: 'It must be in the river, mustn't it?'

Margaret Ann Wiggins was taken to a police station and then driven to Scarborough. Whilst being driven through Malton she pointed to a bridge and said that was where she had dropped Melana into the river. Further questioning gave police the basic outline of what had happened since Dianne Wade left her daughter in her mother's care.

Margaret and Melana had caught the bus to Scarborough and arrived there at four-thirty in the afternoon. They had gone to a cafe and whilst there Margaret appeared unable to cope with her grand daughter. A few hours later they were on a bus heading for Malton, which is about halfway between York and Scarborough. On the bus Melana started crying but Margaret did not have any milk or nappies. It was then, according to her statement, that she decided to do something to Melana. The bus got into Malton shortly after seven and Margaret put Melana into her pushchair and started to push her along. By the time they had got to the bridge Melana was crying and screaming. Margaret put a dummy in Melana's mouth but that did not work. She then picked Melana up and held her above the river (which was about twenty foot below the bridge and four and a half foot deep) before letting go of her.

Margaret then went to a pub and had two drinks of Guinness and played on a fruit machine before catching a bus to Leeds. She then decided to visit a friend who was in hospital in Liverpool so she hitched a lift in a car. When she got to Liverpool she could not find the hospital and ended up sleeping in a station waiting room. The following morning she returned to Leeds and after wandering about approached the police woman.

The case came to trial on Tuesday, 7 July 1974 at York Crown Court. Mr Justice Waller presided, Donald Herrod QC, prosecuted, and Harry Ognall defended Margaret. She pleaded guilty to the manslaughter of Melana and was sentenced to be detained at Broadmoor.

Dr Patrick Joseph Quin, of Clifton Hospital, said that Margaret had a very unstable upbringing. Her father and two sisters had committed suicide; and one of her sons was in Broadmoor following a murder conviction.

Harry Ognall QC, said that there was no criticism of the medical or welfare authorities: 'She was from a family cursed with mental illness to an extent which your Lordship may think is rarely if ever encountered in cases which come before criminal judgement.'

After sentencing, Margaret Wiggins was led from the court moaning: 'No, no, no.' Her daughter, Diane Wade, collapsed and had to be carried from the building.

Chapter 6

George Anthony Morgan

Middlesbrough, 1962
Wakefield, 1975

George Anthony Morgan was gaoled for life in 1975 following a horrendous and vengeful attack on two men in Wakefield, one of whom subsequently died. His previous record of crime included the killing of a drunken man in Middlesbrough, for which he was fortunate to receive only a seven-year sentence; forgery (five years) and wounding with intent (five years).

1. Middlesbrough, 1962
I might have booted him

James Chedzey was a thirty-two-year-old who had been dumb since childhood. He lived in Kingsley Road, Grangetown, Middlesbrough in the North Riding, which became part of Cleveland in 1974. On Thursday 7 June 1962, he had been drinking in the town. Around ten o'clock that evening the women he had been drinking with decided to leave as his drunken behaviour was getting worse. Left on his own, his mood became more unpleasant and aggressive. He left the hotel and decided to try another but the licensee's wife refused him entry. His response was to take off his watch and remove his dentures but the presence of another man seems to have made him change his mind about forcing an entry.

The argument was witnessed by a man standing in the street, who had made no attempt to interfere in the argument. James then turned from the hotel and staggered along the street and turned into another street where he fell against an arch. A man was seen kicking his face and head as he lay on the ground, and then ran off. A few minutes later two youths arrived and an ambulance and the police were called. James was taken to hospital suffering from serious head injuries.

Around twenty minutes later a man walked into the local police station and asked if it was his mate who had been knocked unconscious. The duty officer became suspicious and after a while he asked the man to remain at the police station. Later that morning he was interviewed and he said that he had met James outside the hotel and as they had walked along the street they had argued and he had hit James a few times. The man, George Anthony Morgan, aged nineteen, of Birdsall House, Bodmin Close, Middlesbrough was charged with maliciously causing grievous bodily harm.

On Friday, 22 June, the *Evening Gazette* reported that Morgan had appeared before Middlesbrough Magistrates' Court that day and had now been charged with murder as James had died. The report did not say when he died nor did the report of the trial give a date for his death.

The case came to trial on Wednesday, 27 July 1962 at Newcastle Assizes. Morgan pleaded not guilty to the murder but admitted to a manslaughter charge. The court accepted his plea because of the 'very aggressive mood' of James Chedzey shortly before his death. Mr Bernard Gillis QC outlined the case. After the women had left him in the pub because of his drunken behaviour he had become more aggressive and moody. When he left he went to an hotel but was refused entry, it appeared that he was about to start fighting but the appearance of a man deterred him. Soon after, a man was seen to be stamping on James's head and face. As he rolled away he was kicked in the side, his attacker then continued kicking his face and head. As James lay injured on the pavement his assailant ran off. Morgan returned to the scene with another youth and the police and an ambulance were called.It was then that Morgan made his way to the police station and enquired if it was his mate who had been knocked unconscious. The duty sergeant was suspicious of Morgan and asked him to stay at the station for the night. In a statement he said that he had met James outside the hotel and as they walked away from it they had argued. He had struck James a few times and James had banged his head against an arch. He might have kicked James but he could not remember.

Morgan's counsel, Brian Boyle QC said that it was a sad case. If the manslaughter plea had not been accepted he would have called two witnesses who would have stated that on at least two occasions that evening James had been spoiling for a fight. It was highly likely that his client had been provoked before the fight. He also told the court that James had fallen out of his hospital bed and this could have been the cause of his death, without the fall James might have survived.

Justice Sachs said that the case was 'a dreadful example of the prevalence in the area of using the boot' when drunk. Morgan was sentenced to seven years' imprisonment.

2. Wakefield, 1975
I don't know what made me do it

An anonymous phone call in the early hours of Sunday, 24 August 1975 sent police to a school yard in Brook Street, Wakefield. When they arrived at the old Cathedral School they found two men, unconscious. The men were taken to Pinderfields Hospital where they were treated for serious head injuries. They were soon identified as twenty-two-year old Geoffrey Budby of Walker Avenue, Wakefield who was described as mentally retarded and twenty-five-year-old Dennis Stringer of Coach Road, Wakefield.

The next day, police travelled to Dewsbury and arrested unemployed George Anthony Morgan aged thirty-two of no fixed address. On Wednesday, 27 August he appeared before Wakefield Magistrates charged with causing grievous bodily harm to Dennis Stringer. No application was made for bail and he was remanded in custody. On Monday, 8 September, he appeared before the magistrates and the charge was changed to murder as Dennis Stringer had died on the Sunday, 31 August. A charge of causing grievous bodily harm to Geoffrey Budby was added. Mr J Harrow, who represented Morgan at the hearing, said that he was looking for people who had seen Morgan in the Fleece Inn, Brook Street on the Bank Holiday Saturday evening. Peter Jeffries, prosecuting

Brook Street, Wakefield. The Author

the case, told the magistrates that Morgan's bloodstained clothing had been sent to the forensic laboratory at Harrogate and when questioned about the assault on Dennis Stringer he had made some admissions. Morgan was again remanded in custody.

The case came to trial at Leeds Crown Court on Monday, 26 January 1976 with Justice Thesiger presiding. Morgan denied the murder and grievous bodily harm charges. Mr Geoffrey Baker QC told the court that two men were found injured in the playground of the former Catherdral School in Brook Street, Wakefield in the early hours of Sunday, 24 August. They were unrecognisable due to the extensive violence used against them. Dennis Stringer died the following Sunday. His left ear had nearly been torn off, his nose, jaw and two ribs had been broken. The broken ribs had punctured a lung. He had received extensive head injuries that caused brain injuries from which he never recovered and died without regaining consciousness. Jeffrey Budby's injuries included a fractured eye socket, cheekbone and jaw.

The prosecution case was that Morgan had a grudge against Dennis. In 1969 Mogan had been jailed for uttering forged £5 notes. He believed that Dennis had 'grassed' on him for that offence. In an interview with the police, Morgan had said that when he hurt someone he really hurt them. He thought he needed treatment. When they were knocked out he could not stop, he would carry on, he would pick them up and ram them against something. The prosecution said that Morgan had admitted picking up Dennis and using him as a ramrod. Morgan had then left but decided to go back and look at Dennis. As he did so Jeffrey had followed him and, according to Morgan, Jeffrey had said something so he had dropped him.

When Morgan gave evidence he claimed that Dennis had invited him to fight and Dennis had struck the first two blows. He had defended himself and hit Dennis but he had nothing to do with the assault on Jeffrey. When cross-examined he agreed that Dennis had grassed on him about the forged £5 notes and he had been sent to prison because of it. He denied he had a grievance against Dennis from that time. Dennis had kept pestering him and denying that he had grassed on him. In the pub he had told Dennis to leave him

The Fleece. The Author

alone. They had left the pub and gone into the yard at Dennis's suggestion, he had tried to calm him but Dennis had turned round and hit him so he had defended himself.

Morgan's counsel asked that the jury be shown copies of Dennis and Jeffrey's records, but what was in those records was not made public. The jury were only aware that Morgan had been sent to prison over forged £5 notes. Morgan gave the impression to the jury that he was a quiet man who kept his hands to himself unless he was provoked. He told the court that he did not have an uncontrollable temper. He had hit Dennis in self defence and had not touched Jeffrey.

The jury did not believe Morgan's account and they convicted him of murder. Justice Thesiger sentenced him to life and ordered that the jury be told of his record. Previously, as we have seen, he had been given a seven year sentence for manslaughter, in 1962; but also got five years for wounding with intent when he attacked a man in a Hartlepool flat in 1970, breaking his jaw and some of his ribs. The prison report that said he created situations in which he had to be kept in isolation.

The old Cathedral School, near The Fleece. The Author

Chapter 7

John Robinson

Shipley, 1962
Huddersfield, 1976

John Robinson was released from prison in 1976, despite a judge's recommendation in 1962 that he should be incarcerated for life, for the dreadful killing of a nine-year-old boy. A few months following his freedom – in an apparent jealous rage – he killed and mutilated Mrs Mary Batty in Huddersfield.

1. Shipley, 1962

You must be kept in prison
for the rest of your life

On 23 July 1962, Clive Jones, aged nine and his ten-year-old friend were fishing for tiddlers in the River Aire near an area being developed into an industrial estate later to be called the Dockfield Trading Estate, situated on the outskirts of Shipley. A man called over saying that he had seen rabbits run from the river bank to a nearby wood. Clive went with the man into the wood. A little later Clive's friend heard him cry out and saw the man emerge from the wood alone. Clive's friend ran to Clive's home in Wrose, Bradford and told his parents what had happened. They, and a neighbour, John Armstrong, rushed to the area and searched the wood. It was John Armstrong who found Clive's body in some undergrowth. The boy's throat had been cut.

The police were called and a murder investigation was launched. Clive's friend told the police that the man was between thirty-five and forty, about five foot ten inches, slim with brown hair, dirty teeth; with rough hands and was unshaven. The suspect wore brown shoes, light coloured trousers and a three-quarter length overcoat which had a small brown and white checked pattern but no belt. When this detailed description was made public residents of the Buttershaw area of Bradford named John Robinson, a thirty-three-year-old lorry driver. He was not known as a sex offender to the police but was on bail pending a court appearance for burglary. When police went to Robinson's home he had left but he was traced and arrested in Matlock, Derbyshire, three days later.

Pathologist Dr David Price, conducted the post-mortem and found that the four inch long throat wound had cut both of Clive's jugular veins. He was of the opinion that the weapon used was a small knife like a pen knife. Although Clive's shirt had been undone there was no evidence of a sexual assault.

Whilst being taken back to Shipley, Robinson is alleged to have said that he had met two young lads who were fishing. He had taken one of them into the wood and had 'done him in'.

Robinson was tried at Leeds on Tuesday, 2 October 1962. Barrister Mr A B Boyle said that as Robinson was undoing Clive's shirt, Clive had tried to run off. This had startled him and the penknife he was holding had 'nicked' Clive's neck. He had not explained why he had started to undo Clive's shirt but the jury could draw their own conclusions. His wife had given birth to a boy nineteen days before the murder. In contrast, Mr Boyle QC said that the 'nick' was accidental but the extent of the injury indicated that serious harm was intended and that made the case murder. Whilst on remand Robinson had told another prisoner that he had been drinking and Clive would not have been killed if he had not struggled. A pathologist stated that the nick was four inches long and had severed both jugular veins. His counsel, Mr G W Waller QC, asked a Detective Sergeant to confirm that Robinson had no previous convictions for sexual assaults on children.

Robinson did not give evidence in his own defence. It only took the jury twenty minutes to find him guilty of murder. Justice Finnemore sentenced him to life and added: 'You must be kept in prison for the rest of your life.' Yet Robinson was released less than fourteen years later, in May 1976.

2. Huddersfield, 1976

Not to be released
until the end of your days

Mary Batty and her husband Thomas had a turbulent marriage. By the summer of 1976 they had been married seven years and both had other partners. Thomas, a twenty-five-year-old textile worker, moved out of the family home in Whitacre Close, Deighton, Huddersfield and went to live in Beech Avenue, Golcar. Mary and their son David Adam, aged four, remained in Deighton.

On the afternoon of Saturday, 2 October 1976, Mary's boyfriend, thirty-year-old Gavin Coldwell of Back Firth Street, Rastrick, Brighouse, called to see her. He saw that the downstairs curtains were still drawn. He could hear young David crying. The sound seemed to come from behind the front door. Lifting the letterbox, he spoke to David, and what the lad said caused him grave concern. David told him that his mummy was lying on the floor 'bleeding'. Gavin went to the back door, kicked it open and, after entering, found Mary's body. It was a ghastly sight that lay before him. Mary had her house-coat and underwear on but her body had been mutilated. He alerted a neighbour about the

Whitacre Close, Deighton, Huddersfield. The Author

situation and the police were soon on the scene. Gavin was taken in for questioning but was released after seven hours because the police had a far better suspect for the murder.

On the previous evening, Mary and neighbour Janet Bentley, had met John George Robinson who was the uncle of Thomas Batty, at Huddersfield Bus Station. They went to the *Commercial* before returning to Deighton and calling at the *Little John* for the last drinks where they met up with Janet's husband, Billy. They decided to go to Mary's for supper and arrived there at about quarter to twelve, having picked David up from a neighbour on the way. After eating supper the Bentleys left at half-past twelve, leaving Mary, David and John at the house. Later that morning, the people who lived next door to Mary heard the sound of an argument but assumed she was rowing with her husband.

Mrs Helen Wilson, Mary's twin sister, helped the police when they questioned young David about his mother's murder. He told them that the man in the house had blood on his face. David was taken to his father's home and was given a police guard just in case the killer decided to silence him.

A description of forty-seven-year-old John George Robinson was issued. He was white, 6 foot 2 inches tall, working as a labourer, with dark, greying hair. The clothes he was last seen in were a dark blue raincoat and trousers, a white patterned shirt with brown tie and brown shoes.

Robinson was born in Durham and still had strong ties to the area. The police used tracker dogs to search the canal bank that ran between Whiteacre Close and Leeds Road but they would not disclose what they were looking for.

On the Tuesday night, police found Robinson when they searched the brickyard where he worked. They had been searching the yard each night as Robinson could not return to his home in Dickinson Street, Wakefield. On the next day, he was charged with Mary's murder and remanded in custody. That same day, children found the murder weapon on a railway embankment near Red Doles Road, almost a mile from her home, by the Huddersfield Broad Canal.

On Monday, 24 January 1977, John George Robinson appeared at Leeds Crown Court. He pleaded guilty to the charge of murder.

Looking along the old filled-in railway cutting behind Whitacre Close. The Author

Mr Gilbert Gray QC told the court that during their enquiries the police had contacted the probation service about Robinson's character and attitude but they had not been of much assistance. The Director of Public Prosecutions had written to the Home Office during the enquiry to find the reasons for Robinson's release from his life sentence, despite the natural life sentence imposed by Justice Finnemore in October 1962. He had received a letter dated 19 January 1977. In this it was stated that the parole board reached its decision based on the provisions of section 63 of the *Criminal Justice Act* of 1967. The relevant parts were contained in paragraphs four and five which the Home Office did not want making public. Mr Gray then handed the letter to Justice Boreham. He then outlined the prosecution case. Robinson had first met Mary when his mother had brought her to visit him in prison. Her mother had done that because she was going to marry his nephew. Once Thomas and Mary had married they would both visit him in prison. Following David's birth they would sometimes take him along on the prison visits.

In 1976, Robinson had been released from prison to an approved hostel in Liverpool. After a while he found a job in Wakefield and moved there, but it was a condition of his release that he did not go to Shipley or Bradford. He started visiting the Battys most weekends and continued to visit Whitacre Close – even after Thomas had moved out. He would send letters to Mary. In one of them he wrote: 'I can not stay at your home any more. I love you and have done since my mother brought you to see me.' In another letter he said that he had 'had enough' of Huddersfield and 'for Mary to give David a kiss from me,' as he would miss seeing him. He also thanked his 'bonny lass' (Mary) for her help. Mr Gray said that there was no indication that there was anything sexual between Mary and Robinson.

It was repeated that on Friday, 1 October 1976, Mary and Janet had met Robinson at Huddersfield Bus Station and they had gone drinking in Huddersfield before all three returned to Deighton. Meeting up with Janet's husband at the Little John the foursome left at last orders to collect David and go to Mary's for supper. Janet and her husband left at about half-twelve in the morning. Mary and David had gone to bed upstairs and Robinson had settled down on the settee. Around two o'clock that morning Robinson had gone up to the bedroom where Mary was in bed with David. Robinson had lifted up the bedclothes. This caused Mary to wake up and shout at him. One of the neighbours was sure that the male voice was Mary's husband (but he was at his own home). To silence Mary, Robinson strangled her. The commotion had woken David but Robinson had been able to get him off to sleep again. Robinson then carried Mary's body downstairs to the living room. There, on the floor, he attempted intercourse but failed. He went to the kitchen for a knife and started to mutilate Mary's body but he bent the blade due to his rage. He returned to the kitchen for a bigger knife, in order to continue the mutilation. Removing parts of her body, he placed them in a plastic bag.

Robinson took Mary's watch and a little over £20 from the house when he left early that morning. He also took the bag containing the body parts, hiding it and its contents in a hedge on Whitacre

Street, at the start of Whitacre Close. Robinson fled to Ferryhill in County Durham where he went drinking. A woman put him up for the night and Robinson gave her Mary's watch. He then returned to the Wakefield area where he was arrested during a search.

In his statement to the police, Robinson claimed that he had done it because he was jealous of Mary's boyfriend Gavin, who he did not like. If he could not have Mary then no one else should have her.

Robinson's counsel, Mr Lewis Lawton QC, said that a consultant psychiatrist described his client as a sadistic, sexual deviant for whom there was no known treatment and he would remain an extreme threat to women until such time as his sex drive is diminished by old age. Mr Lawton said the explanation for the crime would be found in the doctor's report not in Robinson's 'jealousy excuse'. Robinson was thirty two when he killed Clive Jones in 1962 and before that he had served his country in Africa, Hong Kong and on active service in Korea. When he finished his service he was given a 'good character' reference.

Justice Boreham sentenced Robinson to life saying: 'In your case the sentence of life imprisonment means life imprisonment and you shall not be released before the end of your days.' John Robinson died from cancer in April 1980.

Chapter 8

Peter Dunford

Crawley, 1963
Wakefield Prison, 1964

Peter Dunford, aged seventeen, pleaded guilty for the fatal stabbing of a fellow Fascist gang member, Francis Crayton, also seventeen, at his trial at Lewes, Sussex in December 1963. Detained 'At Her Majesty's Pleasure' in the high security Wakefield Prison, Dunford and two other inmates killed prisoner Terence Buckingham in August 1964. Sentenced to death by Justice Howard, Dunford escaped execution since the verdict coincided with the second reading of the bill to abolish capital punishment.

1. Crawley, 1963
He wanted to impress the group

Rivalry between two Fascists led to two murders in different counties. The first murder occurred at Crawley in Sussex. The incident occurred at lunchtime on Wednesday, 2 October 1963, in Crawley's main shopping area, The Broadway. Shoppers had reported a fight between two youths and Police Sergeant Peter Cooke had gone to investigate. Arriving at the scene, he encountered a crowd. Making his way through the crowd he saw a youth lying on the floor. He was face down and a knife was sticking out of his back, near his shoulder. Sergeant Cooke recognised the youth as Francis Gerald Crayton, a seventeen- year-old apprentice marine engineer from Langley Green, Crawley. He knew Francis as he had earlier been called to the club where the young man used to go.

When the ambulance arrived Sergeant Cooke helped get Francis on board and rode with him to the hospital. Once medical staff decided that the knife could be removed, Sergeant Cooke retained it as evidence. The doctor held out little hope for Francis' survival as the knife had caused serious damage to his spinal cord.

The investigation soon focused upon youths of the local British Union Movement. That afternoon, they were all rounded up except for one who had gone to the police station shortly after the incident and confessed to the crime. Initially, they thought he had witnessed the fight and decided to confess for the publicity. The other youths who had been apprehended were soon telling the police that there had been a power struggle within their group.

The youth who had confessed was Peter Dunford, a seventeen-year-old labourer who lived in Beckett Lane, Langley Green. Six foot tall, Dunford had founded the local branch of the British Union Movement. His family said he had started the group in a bid to make himself 'look important' and cover up his shyness.

The police knew of the rivalry between the two factions because Francis had been let off with a warning after he pleaded guilty to assault following an incident in July. Francis and some of his supporters within the group had thrown petrol bombs at Dunford and two of his 'clan'. In an attempt to impress the group's girls, Dunford had started to spend money in September. Dunford had decided that he could regain leadership of the group by eliminating Francis. He brought a sheath knife that had a ten inch blade and sharpened it so it had two cutting edges.

When questioned by the police Dunford said that he knew Francis had lunch at a cafe in Crawley so he had waited for him to leave. He had then gone up to Francis in a friendly manner. They had joked about the petrol bomb attack and parted company. Dunford had then followed Francis and stabbed him in the back – in front of the shoppers – as he wanted to scare the rest of the group. He had then made his way to the police station to confess to the stabbing. Dunford appeared at a special court sitting that evening, charged with the wounding.

On Friday, 4 October, at Crawley Hospital, Francis died due to the knife wound. An inquest was held at Horsham the following Tuesday. Dunford was then charged with murder. Francis was buried at Snell Hatch cemetery in the town. At the service, Father

G Williams told the congregation that, as Catholics: 'We have no option but to pray for both of these boys. There is no room here for feelings of vindictiveness.'

On Friday, 9 December 1963, Dunford appeared before Justice Barry at Lewes Assizes. The trial only lasted four minutes as he pleaded guilty to the murder charge. Speaking on his behalf, his counsel Malcolm Morris QC, said that Dunford had not tried to blame anyone else nor make excuses for the crime. He fully realised that what he had done was very wrong and he was sincerely sorry. Justice Barry then sentenced him to be detained until Her Majesty's Pleasure be known. Before the case had come to trial the youths of the local branch of the British Union Movement had disbanded it.

Within nine months, Dunford had killed again, this time in Yorkshire.

2. Wakefield Prison, 1964
Today's the day

On the afternoon of Saturday, 22 August 1964, Terence John Buckingham, a twenty-year-old prisoner had been playing football. After the game he changed back into his prison clothes and returned to his cell on C wing in Wakefield Prison. At five to four a prison officer found him badly injured and he was rushed to Clayton Hospital but died soon after arrival. His death had been caused by head injuries and three stab wounds. Detective Inspector Kenneth Oakley who was put in charge of the investigation set up a murder investigation office in the prison and his team from Wakefield City Police CID interviewed various prisoners. He told the press that a murder in prison has certain advantages and disadvantages for the investigating officer. The suspects were already in custody but they seldom gave truthful answers when questioned.

Terence was described as a labourer and motor dealer, from Notting Hill, London. At the Old Bailey on 26 November 1963 he had been sentenced to four years for the robbery of an eighty-year-old tobacconist. In January, he had been paroled from Wormwood Scrubs so that he could marry. In February, he had been

The main entrance, Wakefield Prison. The Author

transferred to Wakefield Prison. He had been battered over the head and stabbed three times in the back.

A metal bar was found in Terence's cell and was this that had been used to batter him. A prisoner named Carpenter had found a knife, a dagger and a bloodstained towel in his cell and notified prison officers. The knife and dagger had no blood on them and the police did not regard them as potential murder weapons. In another cell a bloodstained pair of grey prison trousers were found but its inmate was eliminated from enquiries. A search of the prison yard resulted in a bloodstained vest and shirt being found. The enquiries resulted in three prisoners from C Wing being charged with murder. They were Peter Anthony Dunford, an eighteen-year-old labourer from Crawley in Sussex; Roy John Powell, a twenty-year-old capstan operator from Birmingham and Michael Martin Morgan, a twenty-one-year-old engineer from Nottingham. In mid-November, when the inquest was resumed, it was adjourned again, pending the outcome of the court case.

The trial started at Leeds on Monday, 7 December 1964. Justice Howard presided and Henry Scott, QC, prosecuted. The prosecution case was that all three were involved in the murder. Scott said that on Saturdays the prison was more like a club than a prison: inmates could mingle, play music, watch or play football. The jury would hear evidence that there was bad blood between the three accused and Terence. Dunford and Powell had both been hit by Terence and Morgan had had a quarrel with him. Another prisoner would state he had seen Dunford with a knife. A prisoner would describe that whilst he was in the foundry toilet he overheard Dunford utter threats against Terence. Mr Scott, QC showed the court an iron bar and said that it was used in the foundry and was called a wrapping spike. He expressed concern that prisoners could acquire one.

Prisoners gave evidence that Dunford hid an iron bar, from the prison foundry, in his pillow case. One of those prisoners would say that the day before the murder, he had overheard Powell and Dunford talking together, recalling the ominous words: 'Today is the day.'

After Mr Scott finished outlining the Crown's case, witnesses were called. A prisoner said that on the afternoon of the killing he had seen Terence return to the wing after the football match. Terence had gone up to his own landing. Shortly afterwards, he had seen Dunford and Powell leave Terence's cell. Powell had turned into a nearby recess and within seconds he had returned to his own cell. On leaving Terence's cell, Dunford had separated from Powell and he appeared to be holding something in his jacket. Dunford also went into a recess before he went to his own cell. After a minute, he had come out of his cell and looked around the landing before returning to his cell. Soon after, he emerged from his cell wearing a different pair of trousers and went to another prisoner's cell – but quickly returned to his own cell again.

A former prisoner, referred to as 'J' was shown the alleged knife used in the murder said he had made it as a throwing spike for Tony Dunford and that he saw Dunford wrap cord round it so it looked like a dagger. Prisoner 'B' said that more than a week before Terence's death he had been talking to Dunford who had told him that Terence had hit him – so he was going to get him. The same prisoner had seen Terence hit Morgan three times, roughly ten days before the former's death. Prisoner John Cook said that he had seen an iron bar in the bath house on Friday, 21 August. It was in another prisoner's possession but he refused to name him, someone who was not one of the accused. He had seen that prisoner give the bar to Dunford who wrapped it up in his pillow case before leaving the bath house.

Powell denied that he had anything thing to do with Terence's death. On Friday, 11 August Dunford gave evidence. Asked by his counsel, Mr G F P Mason QC, if he had murdered Terence he replied: 'No, sir.' Dunford said that he had never threatened Terence nor did he feel any ill will towards him. During cross-examination, Mr Scott asked Dunford if he thought that the various prisoners who had given evidence against him had got together and perjured themselves. When asked if he thought he had been framed for the murder he replied to the effect that was the impression he had got. He claimed that his bloodstained clothes must have been worn by someone else because he had not worn them that day, Dunford was six foot three inches tall, so they would not have fitted many other prisoners. Mr G Mason claimed that Dunford was wholly innocent, wrongly accused and framed. Morgan denied that he was the look-out man as witnessed by another prisoner. Mr G Gray, for Morgan, said that the prison was a rough place but people there deserved more than rough justice. Mr C Chapman, representing Powell, said that no bloodstains had been found on his clothes, that the accused was locked in his cell at the time of the killing and was Terence's friend. The jury, judge and counsel visited Wakefield Prison on Monday, 14 December. The prosecution finished their case that afternoon.

Justice Howard's summing up took six and a half hours. On 17 December 1964, after two hours and twenty minutes, the jury found all three accused guilty of murder. Morgan and Powell were sentenced to life. The jury were then asked to decide if Dunford was guilty of capital murder under Section 6 of the *Homicide Act 1957*, having committed murder on two separate occasions in Britain. Dunford had pleaded guilty at Lewes Assizes on 9 December 1963. Justice Howard sentenced him to death. He was

The high-security walls, Wakefield Prison. The Author

not executed because a few days later the Commons gave the bill to abolish capital punishment its second reading.

In April 1965, Roy Powell's conviction was quashed by the Court of Appeal. Edward Brownlie who was a prisoner at Wakefield had given a statement saying that Powell was locked in his cell at the time of the killing. He had been released from prison five days after the murder and the police could not find him when the case came to trial. He was in a hospital in Scotland at the time. Morgan and Dunford both gave evidence to support his appeal.

Chapter 9

Brian Wade

Rotherham, 1966
Nottingham, 1998

> Noise can often be a point of friction between individuals, families and neighbours but seldom results in murder. Brian Wade killed his neighbour with a sledge hammer whilst the latter was asleep in bed on a grim July night near Rotherham. More than thirty years later a disturbed and annoyed Wade struck again, hacking his young neighbour to death with a machette.

1. Canklow, Rotherham, 1966
I'll kill the bloody swine

Edwin Percy Cardwell, a forty-six-year-old Rotherham area steel burner, lived with his wife Betty in Wood View Place, Canklow. In June and July 1966, he had argued with Brian Wade, a twenty-one-year-old machinist, who lived in the same street. The arguments had been about the noise Brian Wade made on his way home from the pub on a night.

On Saturday, 9 July, Edwin went over to protest about the noise and a fight started. Edwin ended up on the floor. Friday, 15 July was the start of Brian Wade's annual holiday and he went out drinking. On his way back home, at five-thirty that evening, he saw Betty Cardwell and threatened her. She reported the threats to the police and an officer gave Brian Wade a warning about his behaviour.

Later on that night, Brian Wade decided to go out drinking again. In one pub the licensee suggested that he had had enough. He left and went to another, and carried on drinking. On his way home another police officer warned him about his behaviour. After the officer had left, Wade decided to go to the police headquarters to complain about the officer. However, when he saw Inspector Robbins he did not make a formal complaint. Then he left and returned home.

In the early hours of Saturday morning, Betty Cardwell was woken up by a noise. Gaining her senses, she thought she had heard the bedroom light being switched off. She switched it on and saw her husband, Edwin with blood on his head. The police and an ambulance were soon on the scene and he was taken to Sheffield Royal Infirmary. It was decided to operate on him but the procedure was stopped. Edwin Cardwell died later that morning. A search of the bedroom had revealed a sledge hammer.

The police did not have to look for the suspect as Brian Wade had gone to a police officer and said: 'It's about a possible murder. I might have killed a man. I had trouble with him last week.' He was then taken to the police station and questioned. Later that Saturday morning Wade appeared at the Magistrates' Court and was remanded in custody, charged with murder.

On Thursday, 21 July, an inquest was opened into Edwin's death. Betty Cardwell told the Deputy Coroner, A B Jackson, that Edwin had been in the forces in the last war and had been working for the Slag Reduction Company for about two years. Pathologist Dr David Price, reported the results of his post-mortem. Edwin had suffered an almost circular fracture to the left side of his skull. Death was due to shock and tearing of the brain caused by a compound fracture of the skull. As criminal charges had been instigated, Mr Jackson adjourned the inquest until November.

The case came to trial at Sheffield Assizes on Monday, 24 October 1966. It only lasted ten minutes as Wade pleaded guilty to murder. Prosecuting counsel, Roderick Smith QC, told the court about the earlier trouble between the two men and the incidents on the Friday night that led up to the murder. In a statement Wade had said that when he had returned home late that night he had told people in the house: 'I'll kill that bloody swine when I get hold of him.' He left the house still angry and, picking up the sledge hammer, crossed over the road and went to Edwin's house. He shoulder charged the door and went upstairs where he saw Edwin and Betty asleep in bed. He struck Edwin's head several times with the sledge hammer then he dropped it and left the house. It was probably the sound of the hammer dropping that had woken Betty. After leaving the house Wade had gone up to a police officer and handed himself in.

Wade's counsel, John Cobb QC, acknowledged that there was only one sentence that the Judge could pass. Sentencing him to life, Justice Swanwick told Wade that it was a terrible crime committed with a terrible weapon, apparently because he could not stand to be crossed.

Whilst serving his sentence Wade attacked another prisoner and was sentenced to ten years imprisonment for that offence. He was freed on licence in 1984.

2. Radford, near Nottingham, 1998
He hacked Jonathan sixteen times

On Saturday, 17 January 1998, Wade was annoyed because of loud music being played in the flat below his in Burns Street, Radford, Nottingham. He decided to solve the problem by going downstairs and remove the fuse for the flat causing the noise. When the flat was plunged into darkness, twenty-two-year-old Jonathan Abell who was afraid of the dark, went upstairs to unemployed Wade's flat and told him to replace the fuse. He knew Wade had been the one responsible as they had already had several arguments about the noise coming from the flat. The argument became violent and Wade stabbed Jonathan. Leaving him slumped at the doorway, Wade went back into his flat and returned with a machete. He then hacked Jonathan sixteen times with it.

Wade stood trial at Nottingham Crown Court for the murder of another man whose noise was annoying him. Peter Joyce QC prosecuted the case and Charles Wilde QC defended Wade. On Tuesday, 10 November Wade was found guilty of manslaughter and sentenced to life.

Chapter 10

John George Auckland

Cudworth, 1968
Shafton, 1974

This sad case involves the death of two children over a six-year period. In 1968, John Auckland pleaded guilty to manslaughter following the death of his nine-week-old daughter at his Cudworth home. John was still allowed to look after his children but killed another of his baby daughters, at Shafton, in 1974. Once more, he was convicted of manslaughter and the Barnsley Social Services department held an inquiry into the circumstances of the Auckland tragedy.

1. Cudworth, 1968
She interrupted the card game

John Auckland and his wife Barbara lived in Churchfield Avenue, Cudworth, near Barnsley with their nine-week-old daughter Marianne. In the early hours of Monday, 17 June 1968, John and Barbara were in the kitchen playing cards when Marianne started crying. John went upstairs to quieten down his daughter but she would not stop crying. When his attempts to calm her failed he lashed out. He struck her several times and the violence used proved fatal.

It seems that after killing Marianne, Auckland had decided to make it look like she had suffered her injuries in an accident. Auckland later told the police that he had tripped on the carpet at the top of the stairs and fallen down them whilst he held Marianne; and had been knocked out for a while, probably landing on top of

Churchfield Avenue, Cudworth, near Barnsley. The Author

her. To support this version of events he loosened the nails that held the carpet near the top of the stairs, then waited a while before phoning for help. What Barbara knew about Marianne's death is not clear, there are no reports that she was charged with any crime such as aiding and abetting.

When the case came to court at Leeds Assizes on Tuesday, 15 October 1968, John George Auckland, aged twenty-four, pleaded guilty to the manslaughter of Marianne due to diminished responsibility. The judge sentenced Auckland to eighteen months' imprisonment.

2. Shafton, 1974
I wouldn't call it a vicious attack

Susan Jennifer Auckland had her first birthday on Wednesday, 27 March 1973. She lived in Queen's Drive, Shafton near Barnsley with her parents, John George Auckland and Barbara, together with a brother, John (aged three) and sister, Mandy (aged two). The next day, Barbara left the family home as there had been problems between John and Barbara for several years. Barbara planned to go to her parents in London with Susan. She had not seen them for nearly ten years and but then decided that turning up with Susan would be too much. She decided, therefore, to place Susan into the care of Social Services. The supervision of the Auckland family passed from the West Riding County Council's Social Services Department to Barnsley Metropolitan Borough Council's Social Services Department when the reorganisation of local government came into effect in April.

With John and Mandy to look after, John decided to move in with his own parents in Cudworth. Social workers decided that Susan could join the rest of the family at her grandparents. Her grandmother decided to go on holiday so Susan was returned to the care of social workers from the 11 April to the 10 May. When Susan rejoined the family, John decided to give up work and return to Queen's Drive to look after the children full-time. Social Services agreed to this arrangement. Despite his previous conviction for killing nine-week-old Marianne in 1968, the Social

Queen's Drive, Shafton, Barnsley. The Author

Services department decided not to apply for a compulsory care order as they considered that there were no grounds that could be established for an order to be granted. From visits made by social workers, it appeared that family, friends and neighbours considered that John was looking after the children well. They were always clean and spotless and well-fed. To get a compulsory care order or supervision order neglect had to be established but as their care had improved the department could not justify applying for either order. Barbara was contacted in London and told that John and the children had moved back to the family home in Queen's Drive but she chose not to return nor seek custody of the children.

John's parents visited daily and social workers called occasionally. On Tuesday, 25 June, Barbara asked a social worker if she could have the children with her for a short while but she was told that it would be impracticable. If she came to Barnsley arrangements could be made so that she could see them. During a visit to Queen's Drive at the end of June, a social worker thought that there was no reason for concern over the safety of the children. Even so, an offer by Social Services to take care of the children on a voluntary basis was declined by John.

In the early hours of Thursday, 10 July, detectives were alerted about the death of Susan Jennifer Auckland. When they questioned John about Susan's death he claimed that whilst he was carrying her he had tripped on the carpet at the top of the stairs and had fallen head-first down the stairs and had been knocked out. When they looked at the carpet it was loose but looking into his background they found that it was the same excuse he had given when Marianne had been killed. The police did not believe him as Susan had suffered many injuries and, after further questioning, John was charged with her murder the next day.

The case started at Sheffield Crown Court on Tuesday, 26 November 1974. Prosecution counsel, Barry Mortimer QC, told the jury that Susan had more than one hundred marks on her body, the oldest about a fortnight old. The injuries included marks to her head, face, neck, both arms and both legs, most of them fresh. She also had bruising around both her split lips and her palate was split behind her front teeth, internal bruising in the stomach and internal bleeding in the skull. Thirty-year-old Auckland had waited two hours before calling for an ambulance, during which time he had kicked up the carpet at the top of the stairs to support his version of how Susan had died. He had later made a statement to the police giving another version of how Susan died.

On the evening of Wednesday, 10 July, as he passed Susan's bedroom, he heard her crying loudly and looking in he saw her stood up in her cot. He had shouted to her to shut up as he did not want John and Mandy waking up. When she failed to stop crying he had slapped her across the face a few times. The last slap knocked her backwards but she still held on to the cot and started screaming. Pathologist, Dr Alan Usher told the court that he thought the injuries to her forehead and ears were linked. He thought that Susan had been held by her ears and had been knocked against something solid like a wall or cot. He said that the injuries were typical of what had become known as the battered baby syndrome. In reply to cross-examination, he agreed that some of the bruises could have been caused by rough handling.

A police officer said that Auckland had said that he was sorry for telling lies at first, because he was frightened. He had said he was not a murderer or a maniac. He had not meant to kill Susan, it was not as bad as it looked. The pressure of looking after the children after his wife had left him in March had caused things to get on top of him. He had been a father and mother to them, he had to do for them and get his own meals ready.

Auckland's counsel, Mr Arthur Myerson QC told the jury that he was not going to argue that Susan's injuries were accidental. It was up to the jury to decide if the criminal offence was either murder or manslaughter. He then called Auckland to the witness box and started to question him.

Auckland said that he would not call it a vicious attack but he did think it was the wrong way to go about it. Mandy did quite a bit of crying and Susan cried a lot. When one started crying it would have a snowball effect. When all three started crying he would slap them. By July the strain of looking after the three children had got to the stage that he would break down crying.

On the night of the 10 July, Susan was in her cot crying. He lost his temper and slapped her across the face. He then put his hands around her neck and shook her hard. He then picked her up to get her a bottle but banged his head on the bedroom door, this dislodged a lens from his glasses and as he bent down to pick it up Susan fell to the floor. He made various attempts to revive her before he went out to call for an ambulance. He admitted that he had kicked up the carpet in an attempt to cover up what had happened.

The jury were not aware of his previous conviction and found him guilty of manslaughter, on Friday, 28 November. Justice Lawson read social and medical reports on Auckland and heard Arthur Myerson QC say that his client recognised that he is not a fit and proper person to have the care and custody of children. Auckland was then sentenced to five years.

Justice Lawson then ordered that Timothy Jones, a social worker for Barnsley District Council, be recalled to the witness box. Justice Lawson then asked Mr Jones if he was aware of Auckland's previous conviction before the decision was made to give him custody of the three children. Mr Jones replied that he was and attempted to say more but Justice Lawson stopped him and said 'Thank you very much, that is all I wanted to know.' Justice Lawson then said that he was going to take steps to see that an inquiry was made, that is why he had asked Mr Jones that question.

On Wednesday, 11 December, the chairman of the Social Services Committee told a Press conference: 'The committee are satisfied, in the light of all the facts presented that the Social Services Department's staff acted properly and responsibly in what were considered to be the best interests of the Auckland family at the time.' A copy of the internal inquiry was sent to the Department of Health and Social Security.

Chapter 11

George Dennis Unsworth

Hong Kong, 1970
Huddersfield, 1980

Huddersfield-born George Unsworth, when serving as a professional soldier in Hong Kong, murdered a prositute. His defence council referred to Unsworth's unstable mental health though this medical situation was denied by a psychiatrist and the Army. Nevertheless, in June 1979, following brain surgery, he was released on license from an English prison. A few months later Unsworth killed an eleven-year-old Huddersfield schoolboy.

1. Hong Kong, 1970

He wanted his change

George Dennis Unsworth was born in Kilner Bank Road, Huddersfield on 9 May 1949, the youngest in a family that included a brother and three sisters. He grew up in Huddersfield and attended junior school before going to Deighton Secondary School. When he was eleven years old, his sixteen-year-old sister, Jeanette, disappeared. Despite the police being involved, she has not been seen or heard from since. As a juvenile George became known to the police as a petty offender. He left school at fifteen and started work as an oat roller at Martins Corn Merchants, in Aspley. He left there after six months and then did a series of jobs as a case-maker, car washer and found work at Dobson's sweet factory. In April 1966, he enlisted in the Huddersfield-based 1st Battalion Duke of Wellington's

Sketch of George Unsworth. Carl Lawson

The old Supreme Court, Hong Kong. The Author

Regiment, serving in Germany and Cyprus. He took up boxing but this came to an end when his drinking got worse. In 1968, he married Susan, a Huddersfield girl. His next posting was to Hong Kong, Susan remaining in Huddersfield. In August 1970 (most report says the 8th one the 17th), Private Unsworth went to the red-light district of Wanchair. He spent his time drinking, then picked up Chan Waichun, a fifty-three-year-old prostitute. He went with her to Jaffe Road and had sex with her on a first floor landing in a block of flats. She asked for 15 Hong Kong dollars (about £1 at that time). He gave her two $10 notes but she refused to give him his $5 change. He then battered her head against a wall and the floor, jumped on her and assaulted her with a broom handle before throwing her body down the stairs.

The *Huddersfield Daily Examiner* dated Tuesday, 18 August 1970, carried a report and photograph of Private Unsworth on its front page. The item said that a telegram from Infantry Records to his parents had that morning notified them that he been charged with murder. The paper carried a report on 23 September saying that magistrates in Hong Kong were into the second day of a hearing into whether or not he should be sent for trial. The hearing was held behind closed doors and was expected to end the next day. The *Examiner* did not report the outcome of the committal proceedings but he was tried later that year.

The trial of Private George Denis Unsworth was held at the Hong Kong Supreme Court in November 1970 and lasted five days. His defence counsel told the court that medical reports indicated he was insane or had suffered an epileptic fit when he killed Chan Waichun. Reference was made to an abnormality in his brain which led to the attack. There were suggestions that he had suffered blackouts, the result of his boxing bouts. He also claimed that the blackouts were due to his being hit on the head with a rifle shortly after joining up. The Duke of Wellington Regiment denied the claim and pointed out that he had never reported sick nor had he claimed to be suffering from any signs of epilepsy. His Army record classified him as an average soldier, a heavy drinker who regularly visited prostitutes.

A psychiatrist, Dr W T Hwang said that Unsworth was not insane when he killed Chan Waichun, that he knew what he was doing and he knew it was wrong. He had not suffered an epileptic fit at the time of the killing as his memory of the event was too good.

Chief Justice Sir Ivor Rigby described the evidence concerning Unsworth's mental health presented by the defence as rather flimsy. Jailing Unsworth to life for the manslaughter of Chan Waichun, Sir Ivor said he would have jailed him for seven years but his apparent personality defects changed his mind as he thought an indeterminate life sentence would be more appropriate. He also said that if Unsworth received medical treatment he could be released early.

After Unsworth was transferred to an English prison he was operated on. He was released on license in June 1979 after officials decided he did not pose a serious risk to the public. Only eight months later he was to prove those officials were wrong when he killed an eight-year-old in Huddersfield.

2. Huddersfield, 1980

Guess my dog's name

At teatime, on Saturday, 9 February 1980, Paul Hinchliffe, aged eleven was telling his father, also called Paul about a man who had offered him and his friends sweets, pears and cigarettes. Paul became more alarmed when his son told him that one of his friends, Andrew Cross, an eight- year-old, had gone with the man to the steps leading to the cellar at Moldgreen Youth Club to smoke a cigarette. Paul decided to go and look for Andrew at the Youth Club in Chapel Street, just off Wakefield Road. When he looked into the cellar he found Andrew's partly clothed body.

Detective Superintendent Alf Finlay was soon launching a major murder inquiry with eighty officers involved. Paul and his two other friends, Colin Bowan, aged eight and Gareth Bowan aged six spoke about the man with a dog who had approached them. The police were looking for a white man of medium build aged from twenty to forty, about five foot eight inches tall. He had long dark brown hair, a tattoo on his chest and a silver medallion on a leather thong which featured two lions. He was wearing National Health spectacles, dirty jeans, a denim jacket and a blue-grey shirt, open to the waist. He had a large fawn and brown unkempt mongrel dog, possibly called Smokey with him.

The police had various reports concerning a similar man seen in the area that afternoon. A motorist had seen a man talking to a group of young boys near the Moldgreen Junior School playground. Two shop assistants at a greengrocer's in Wakefield Road, Moldgreen had served a similar man with a bag of pears that afternoon. On Sunday afternoon, a local man was detained and questioned. The person had been in the area that afternoon with a dog and had visited the greengrocer's shop. It took him more than a day to convince the officers that he was not the man who killed Andrew.

On the Tuesday, officers questioned the occupant of an attic flat in Somerset Road, Almondbury, Huddersfield. He matched the general description, but did not have a dog nor was he wearing glasses; however, the officers noticed that he had marks above the bridge of his nose that indicated he did wear spectacles. A search of

Looking along Chapel Street, Moldgreen, Huddersfield. The Author

the flat revealed stolen knickers and a collection of pornography. Thirty-year-old George Dennis Unsworth was taken in for questioning. His previous manslaughter conviction and crucifix tattoo on his chest added to their suspicions and he was interviewed at length. He was charged with Andrew's murder and remanded in custody.

The case came to trial on Wednesday, 25 September 1980, at York Crown Court. Unsworth pleaded guilty to the murder. Humphrey Potts QC, outlined the background to the case. In June 1971, Unsworth was transferred from Hong Kong, where he was serving a life sentence for the manslaughter of a local woman, to England. In June 1972, he underwent an operation, at Pinderfields Hospital in Wakefield, on his brain. This involved cutting nerve fibres in the frontal lobes to treat his mental condition. The operation appeared to work and in 1974 he was sent to an open prison, and moved four years later to a hostel in Nottingham. The following year he obtained work at a subsidiary of the Raleigh bike company. His progress was deemed to be good so the new Home Secretary, William Whitelaw authorised his release on licence in June 1979. In July he quit his job and moved back to his home town, Huddersfield, renting an attic flat above his parent's in Somerset Road. In August he got a job in nearby Greetland. In November he was caught at Longley Park Golf Club whilst committing a burglary. He pleaded guilty and was fined £150. The Home Office was notified but, despite his previous juvenile convictions for burglary and theft (and the manslaughter conviction) it was decided that this latest offence was dissimilar to his previous convictions, so his licence was not revoked. He was therefore allowed to remain free to murder Andrew three months later.

On Saturday 9 February, George Dennis Unsworth had been drinking with his father then they returned home. George offered to change a jigsaw puzzle that his father had brought for his mother as she already had the puzzle. The shop was in Wakefield Road so George walked there and on the way saw a group of boys in Moldgreen Junior School playground. In a shop he brought some chewing gum, pears and cigarettes. He also came across a stray dog which he kept and met the boys. They got talking about bicycles and George offered the boys the pears and chewing gum. He then offered them some cigarettes and suggested they went behind the youth club so they would not be seen. After a while the boys began to wander away for their tea. When Andrew was the only one left George got him to go into the basement at the youth club. In his interviews with the police he said that Andrew was far to friendly towards a stranger and he wanted to teach him a lesson. Andrew had started to scream so Unsworth put his hand over his mouth and then pulled a scarf tight around his neck, strangling the boy. Unsworth was back home within minutes.

Counsel for Unsworth, Arthur Hutchinson QC, pointed out that reference had been made to the apparent lack of remorse from Unsworth but during his interviews he had expressed remorse. He hoped that his client would be sent to a prison where he would receive treatment. Justice Jupp sentenced Unsworth to life.

Chapter 12

Douglas Wakefield

Leeds, 1974
Parkhurst Prison, 1978

Douglas Wakefield was sentenced to life imprisonment for the murder of his uncle in 1974. Whilst an inmate of Parkhurst, on the Isle of Wight, he killed his cell-mate, another murderer, Brian Peake, saying that he thought he was his uncle.

1. Leeds, 1974

He's gone to Bolton-upon-Dearne

When Derek Wakefield's brother asked his nephew Douglas Wakefield where Derek was he was told that he had gone to his sister's at Bolton-upon-Dearne. On 18 May 1974, his brother rang their sister and she said he had not been to see her lately. Following further enquiries, relatives visited Gipton police station to report their concerns. Derek's disappearance was of interest to the police because he was on bail on a burglary charge. Derek and Douglas were both meant to report to the police each day but Derek had not done so since 3 May.

The police went to Derek's home in Foundry Place, Gipton, Leeds and searched the house and garden. They were suspicious when they saw freshly dug earth in the back garden. Early on the morning of Sunday, 19 May, Derek's body was found, buried three foot deep below the freshly dug earth. On the Monday, Douglas Wakefield, a twenty-seven-year-old unemployed labourer appeared before Leeds magistrates charged with the murder of his uncle, Derek, a forty-three-year-old labourer, at the home they shared.

Foundry Place, Gipton, Leeds. D. Speight

The magistrates were told that Professor David John Gee had conducted a post-mortem. The Professor found that Derek had suffered forty-six stab wounds and compression of the neck. Chief Superintendent Dennis Hoban and Superintendent Jim Hobson had interviewed Douglas at Gipton police station, during which he had admitted killing his uncle. Later on, he made a statement in the presence of his solicitor. Mr Barrington Black, representing Douglas, asked for reporting restrictions to be lifted. The large police presence at their home had led to rumours that there was more than one body and he wanted it made public that the police were satisfied that only one death was involved. Douglas was remanded in custody.

The trial started on Tuesday, 5 November 1974 at Leeds Crown Court. Mr D J Clarkson QC, prosecuted. He told the court that Douglas denied the murder charge and claimed that he killed his uncle because of an argument. When arrested he was alleged to have said that it was murder, he could not even say it was manslaughter, as he had had it in his head to kill someone since March. Later, he had claimed that the killing was not premeditated but the result of his uncle provoking him. Douglas had told Derek that he wanted a sex change and wanted to carry out a robbery to pay for it. Derek had made fun of him so he had attacked him. Derek was strangled with a belt, attacked about the head with an hammer then stabbed about the head and upper body with a garden fork.

Mr Clarkson told the jury that there could be another reason for the murder. At eleven-thirty on the night of 10 April a police officer responded to a radio message to attend an incident. At a phone box near Douglas' home he saw two youths, one of whom, Eric Dinsdale, had a stab wound in his shoulder. The officer went to Douglas' home and saw Derek, and later saw Douglas, arresting him on a wounding charge. It was claimed that he said his uncle had 'grassed' on him. Following Douglas' arrest, a search was made of the house and two ornaments matching the description of two stolen from a nearby shop were found. Douglas said Derek had stolen them but the police thought Douglas was involved so they were both charged with burglary. Mr Clarkson told the jury that Douglas' guilt or innocence on the burglary and wounding charge was not their concern.

On Thursday, 7 November, Douglas Wakefield was sentenced to life for the murder of his uncle.

2. Parkhurst Prison, 1978

It was his uncle, not Brian that he killed

In 1978, Douglas Wakefield was four years into his life sentence for the murder of his uncle in Leeds. He was in Parkhurst Prison on the Isle of Wright. On the evening of Wednesday, 20 September, a prisoner looked into Wakefield's cell and saw him looking at the wall. The prisoner then saw another prisoner laying on the cell floor with blood on him. He then raised the alarm and prison officers rushed to the cell.

Douglas was removed from the cell and told the prison governor that he had killed 'his uncle Derek'. The dead prisoner was in fact Brian William Peake, aged thirty eight. He was also serving a life sentence for murder. He had been convicted of the sex murder of Victoria Jane Cummings, a nineteen-year-old nurse who he had attacked in Heath Road, Darlaston, Walsall in Staffordshire on 4 December 1966. Peake was convicted at Stafford Assizes on Thursday, 27 April 1967 and sentenced by Justice Stable – to life imprisonment.

When Wakefield's cell was searched a piece of wood with nails in both ends was found. There was blood on this home-made weapon. When interviewed again, Wakefield said that his uncle had come into his cell and he had gone berserk and killed him. He said he had not seen Brian that evening. When they told him that it was Brian who was dead he insisted that it was his uncle he had killed, not Brian. Following an enquiry by the police, Wakefield was charged with murder.

The case was heard at Winchester Crown Court on Wednesday, 11 April 1979. The prosecution case was presented by Charles Fletcher-Cooke QC. Wakefield pleaded not guilty to the murder charge but his plea of guilty to manslaughter on the grounds of diminished responsibility was accepted. He was then sentenced to a concurrent life sentence. He has now been released from his two life sentences as he has served the twenty year tariff that he was given.

Chapter 13

John Paton

Wakefield Prison, 1976
Parkhurst Prison, 1981

Robert Houson received a violent death in the hands of fellow prison inmate John Paton in 1976 was given a life sentence. Paton killed again about five years later, this time in Parkhurst Prison on the Isle of Wight. The victim was Belfast-born Frank McGee. Paton hanged himself in Garth Prison, Leyland in 1997.

1. Wakefield Prison, 1976
It wasn't the horses, it was the hooch

Mrs Joan Houston, aged forty-six, from Clayton-le-Moors, Lancashire, visited her twenty-three-year-old son, Robert Houston, at Wakefield Prison. He was serving a six-year prison sentence for robbing a man in Accrington. By September 1976 he was two years into his sentence and he hoped to be paroled in the following March. When his mother visited him she would pass him a pound or two. After a while he asked her for more because he owed money to a bookie in the prison. He was frightened but he never told her how much he owed.

Robert Houston had left school at fifteen to start an apprenticeship as a bricklayer but it did not work out. He got a job in a tailor's shop but quit that when his friends said it was an effeminate job. He then drifted in and out of employment. He married and had a daughter called Zoe who was aged three in September 1976. Her grandmother used to take her to visit Robert at Wakefield Prison but this stopped when her daughter-in-law applied for a divorce and moved.

In mid-September, Mr and Mrs Houston were visited by a police officer who informed them that Robert had been attacked in Wakefield Prison. They travelled to Wakefield to be at his hospital bedside. Robert had suffered head injuries and underwent surgery on Thursday, 23 September. To reduce pressure on his brain a piece of bone was removed during the operation. More surgery was undertaken to try and save him. His parents stayed at the hospital until Robert died on Tuesday, 5 October.

The police investigation into the assault on Robert became a murder investigation led by Detective Superintendent Leonard Shakeshaft. He told a press conference that the earlier inquiry into the assault had uncovered a motive but he would not disclose it. Robert's cell was No. 40 on B wing. On the morning of Tuesday, 14 September, he staggered out of it shortly after it was unlocked. He made his way along the landings then sat on the stairs leading to the next landing, and prison officers went to his assistance. His head injuries were serious so he was taken to Pinderfields Hospital in Wakefield, which had a neurological unit. Few prisoners were willing to help the police inquiry but after Robert's death more information was provided. John Paton, aged forty, serving a nine year sentence for burglary and possession of a firearm and within five years of release from jail, was charged with the murder of Robert Houston.

The case came to trial at Leeds Crown Court on Monday, 21 November 1977, before Justice Pain. John Paton denied the charge. The prosecution case was outlined by John Taylor QC. Counsel for Paton, John Hugill QC informed the court that his client had dispensed with his services and his solicitor's. As there were about 500 pages of evidence the trial was adjourned so the Paton could read them and prepare his own defence. On the Wednesday Paton changed his plea to guilty and Justice Pain sentenced him to life for the murder. He was brought back to court again on the following day because Justice Pain had forgotten to formally take the verdict from the jury once the plea had been changed. Paton then changed his plea to not guilty and a new trial before another jury was started.

John Taylor QC once again outlined the prosecution case and

requested that the identity of the prisoners giving evidence should not be disclosed by the media. Justice Pain endorsed his request. As noted, Robert Houston had been attacked soon after the cells had been opened on B wing on the morning of Tuesday, 14 September. He had been subjected to a brutal attack about his head with a bed leg. Paton's cell was No. 12 on the same landing as Robert's. At six-fifty that morning the cells had been unlocked, prisoner 'C', on the top landing B4, had reported sick and was returning to his cell when he saw Paton going into a recess at the side of Robert's cell. Prisoner 'C' went along his landing to cell No. 14 for a light for his cigarette. As he looked down from the landing he saw Paton looking through the spy hole into Robert's cell. When he had got his light he returned to his cell but saw no sign of Paton when he looked down.

Prisoner 'H' had a cell nearly opposite to Robert's, he had seen Paton in the recess and there was something (it looked like a length of pipe) sticking out of his pocket. At about ten past seven, as he was shaving, in his mirror he saw Paton entering Robert's cell. A few minutes later he saw Paton coming out of the cell. He then saw Robert going along the landing with Paton walking with him.

Prisoner 'F' was in a recess shortly after seven. When he looked down he saw Paton coming out of the cell, holding something in his hand, like a vest or towel. Paton was shouting for a prison officer as he accompanied Robert along the landings.

Paton cross-examined a prisoner who claimed that the reason Paton had attacked Robert was because Robert had stolen some 'hooch' that Paton had brewed. The prisoner had told the police that 'hooch' (alcohol made from potato peelings and fruit) and not a gambling debt was the cause of the problem. Paton accused him of framing another prisoner but he denied it. He told Justice Pain that this trial was a frame-up and gigantic farce. Since he was conducting his own defence, Justice Pain told him that he must 'keep cool'. The prisoner claimed that at the time of Robert's death, Paton was the top 'hooch' man in Wakefield.

John Taylor told the court that Paton did try to summon prison officers and tried to assist Robert as he went along the landings but Robert kept pushing him away. He also showed the jury a table leg that was found in Robert's cell. As Robert sat on the stairs, prison officers soon saw he had serious head injuries. He was sent to hospital and was operated on but he died on Tuesday, 5 October. A pathologist found that he died from meningitis caused by the injuries or surgery.

Paton chose not to give evidence but he told the jury that he had originally pleaded guilty because he took fright: 'It doesn't mean anything to me, imprisonment.' Robert was his friend and had not stolen his 'hooch' nor had he bludgeoned him.

On Friday, 2 December 1977, the jury retired to consider its verdict and found him guilty of murder. Justice Pain sentenced Paton to life, making no recommendation as to a minimum period of detention as it was to run consecutively with his current sentence. In his view it was a brutal murder and the authorities should bear in mind that he should be detained for a substantial period of time. As Paton was led from the dock he called out: 'I didn't do it, my Lord.'

2. Parkhurst Prison, 1981
It happened in the breakfast queue

In August 1978, Francis McGee was sentenced at the Old Bailey to six years imprisonment for robbery, causing grevious bodily harm and burglary. When he was killed by a fellow inmate at Parkhurst Prison on the Isle of Wright in 1981 it barely got a mention in the press. This was despite his killer having being a convicted killer.

There is a report in the Isle of Wright County Press on the opening of the inquest into McGee's death. It was held on Tuesday 14 July 1981 in Newport before coroner Mr J S K Chesterton. Pathologist Dr N Greenwood told the inquest that Home Office pathologist Dr P Pullar carried out a post-mortem on Francis McGee. There were various wounds and lacerations but it was a three quarter of an inch deep knife wound to the heart that killed him.

The senior medical officer at Parkhurst Prison, Dr G Stewart told the inquest that at twenty-past seven on the morning of Friday, 10 July he had gone to C wing after a request for medical treatment was received. He saw Francis being given oxygen by prison staff as he lay at the bottom of some stairs. When he examined Francis he found that he had died. Dr Stewart said that Francis had been worried about what would happen to him when he was discharged. This had made him anxious so he had been prescribed tranquillisers.

A solicitor, Mr P Rickstold the inquest that he was there because he was representing someone who could be concerned with Francis' death. Detective Sergeant W Berry said that a person was likely to be charged with a serious offence in relation to the death of Francis. The inquest was adjourned *sine die* as a trial was likely to be held.

John Paton, serving life for murder, was charged with the murder of thirty-two-year-old Belfast-born Francis McGee.

John Paton, aged forty-six had been convicted of the manslaughter of Francis at Winchester Crown Court on Tuesday, 16 February 1982 and sentenced to life. Paton had stabbed Francis nine times with a piece of tapered steel as they queued for breakfast on C wing. Why he did this is not known. Whether he pleaded guilty to manslaughter is not clear as there appears to be no coverage of the trial. The local Winchester paper did not carry a report nor did the Isle of Wight paper. Although he was Belfast-born there was no coverage in the paper there which is no surprise as it had its own problems at the time. The paper covering Accrington, where his first victim came from, did not report his second conviction.

John Paton, aged sixty-one was found dead in his single cell in Garth Prison, Leyland on Thursday, 28 August 1997. He had been found hanging from a ligature made from torn sheeting when his cell was unlocked in the morning. A prison spokesman said that there were no suspicous circumstances surrounding his death but an inquiry would be held.

Chapter 14

Robert John Mawdsley

(London, 1974)
Broadmoor Hospital, 1977
Wakefield Prison, 1978

Based on his record of killing, Robert Mawdsley is potentially one of the most dangerous prisoners of modern times. In 1977 he was a patient in Broadmoor, having a conviction for manslaughter after the killing of thirty-year-old John Farrell. With fellow inmate David Cheesman, Mawdsley abducted another patient, David Francis, subjecting him to a variety of violence, culminating in a fatal garrotting. Both men were given life sentences. Fifteen months later, unhappy with Wakefield Prison, Mawdsley killed two more prison inmates.

1. Broadmoor Hospital, 1977
Why don't you kill me John?

David Francis, aged twenty-six, was a patient in Broadmoor Hospital. On Saturday, 26 February 1977, there had been a football match between inmates. After the match David was taken hostage in the locker room by two other prisoners, David Cheesman and Robert John Mawdsley. They were both patients in the high security Somerset House wing of the hospital. Nurses at the hospital tried forcing their way into the room when they realised what was happening but Mawdsley pushed against the door to stop them gaining entry. More nurses were available to force the door but when they tried they stopped when they saw Cheesman holding a knife-like object to David's neck. Cheesman then shouted at them to get out as he had a blade. Mawdsley then secured the door.

The two men tied David to a chair and began telling the

Entrance, Broadmoor Hospital. The Author

authorities what they wanted. Their demand to see a psychiatrist and a later demand to see another patient were refused. David was subjected to beatings and torture by the pair, even electric shocks. Later in the siege the sounds of a beating could be heard coming from the room and David was heard shouting: 'Why don't you kill me John?' After ten hours, a gurgling noise and what sounded like feet drumming the floor – as if some one was being strangled – was heard. When the authorities entered the room they found that David had been garrotted. The killing of a patient at Broadmoor Hospital by two fellow patients was not deemed newsworthy and there was very little media coverage of the incident.

On 13 October 1977, the *Bracknell News* carried a report on the Cheesman/Mawdsley trial held at Reading Crown Court. It took place on 6 October before Justice Purchas; prosecuting counsel was Mr Daniel Hollis QC. Cheesman was defended by Ian Davidson QC but Mawdsley's counsel was not mentioned in the report. They both pleaded guilty to the charge of murder. Daniel Hollis outlined the details of the case to the court. Ian Davidson explained that Cheesman had committed the crime to ensure he was moved from Broadmoor Hospital. He explained that several patients regarded murder as their passport out of the hospital.

Justice Purchas sentenced them both men to life imprisonment saying: 'It is clear to me that both of you are extremely dangerous men and there is little hope of any kind of rehabilitation. It is my duty to say this is a case where the Home Secretary should take action under the Mental Health Act to achieve a transfer of each of you to a proper establishment under conditions of maximum security.'

At the end of the hearing Cheesman stood in the dock and told the court that he was prepared to kill again if he was sent back to Broadmoor Hospital by the Home Secretary. He said: 'I have vowed that I should again appear before this court on a like indictment. This is not a threat, but a statement.'

The Bracknell News report gave most of its coverage to Cheesman. It did not report that Mawdsley was in Broadmoor Hospital because he was serving a sentence for manslaughter. It is not clear if this was mentioned in the court or if the reporter thought it was of no importance.

When he was twenty, Robert John Mawdsley had appeared at the Old Bailey on the 26 June 1974. He was convicted of manslaughter due to diminished responsibility and was ordered to be detained without time limit in a secure hospital. He had killed fellow homosexual John Farrell, a thirty-year-old Welshman. The incident occurred in Wood Green, London on 14 March 1974. The local paper, the Wood Green Weekly Herald, carried 4 small reports on 22 March and 5, 12 and 26 April, stating that Robert John Mawdsley had been charged with the murder of John Farrell and remanded in custody. The local paper carried no report on the trial nor did any other paper report it. Several years later, different newspapers gave different versions of what happened. Some claimed he stabbed John, others claim John was garrotted. John died due to loss of blood not asphyxiation.

Mawdsley was six foot two inches and was born in Liverpool on 26 June 1953. He is alleged to have had a disturbed upbringing. Taken into care before he was a year old, he was later returned to his parents. When he was six he was again returned to care.

2. Wakefield Prison, 1978
He wanted to be moved

On Saturday 29 July 1978, Robert John Mawdsley went into the A Wing office at Wakefield Prison. Placing a home-made bladed instrument on the desk, he told the prison officers there that there would be two short at roll call. A prison officer asked him what he meant. Mawdsley replied that he had killed them. The officers took his claim seriously as he was serving a life sentence for a murder committed whilst he was serving a sentence for manslaughter. The officers then went to Mawdsley's cell and found the body of a prisoner under the bed. The victim was Salney Darwood, a forty-six-year-old from Luton who was serving life for manslaughter. On 26 May 1977, he had strangled his wife Blanche, aged fifty-one, at their home in Luton. He pleaded guilty to manslaughter due to diminished responsibility at St Albans Crown Court on the 31 October 1977. Along with stab wounds, Darwood had been garrotted.

In another cell they found William Roberts, a fifty-five-year-old from Sheffield, he was seriously wounded and was rushed to Wakefield's Pinderfields Hospital. William had been stabbed and had suffered head injuries. His wife, Doreen, lived in Fife Gardens,

Wakefield Prison walls. The Author

Wincobank, Sheffield. The police informed her that William had been involved in an accident. She heard a news report on the radio and realised that it was not an accident. William had been sentenced in 1976 to seven years for attempting to choke a four-year-old girl in order to rape her. At Pinderfields Hospital, William was put on a life support machine but eighteen hours after he was admitted he died.

The double murder in Wakefield received very little coverage in the weekly Wakefield Express. There was a small report on 8 August that said Robert John Mawdsley, a twenty-seven-year-old native of Liverpool appeared at Wakefield Court on Tuesday accused of the murder of two fellow prisoners. It named his victims, the presiding magistrate Mr George Wakenshaw, the prosecutor Mr Granville Ropley and Mawdsley's solicitor George Towell. Mawdsley was remanded until the 30 August.

The Sheffield Star on Monday 31 July carried the murders as their main front page report, continuing over on to page seven. It included two photographs, one of William and a smaller one of Doreen. The report said that detectives were expected to complete their enquiries that day. They were questioning a former Broadmoor Hospital patient who had taken another patient hostage and then killed him, this had happened four years previously; the report was wrong on this point, the Broadmoor Hospital incident had occurred the previous year (the incident that happened four years before was the London killing). The next day it carried a report that Mawdsley had been charged.

At Leeds Crown Court on Friday 16 March 1979, Robert John Mawdsley, handcuffed to one prison officer and surrounded by five more officers, appeared before Justice Cantley. He pleaded guilty to murdering Salney Darwood and William Roberts. Mawdsley was given a life sentence for each murder.

Prosecution counsel, Mr Barry Mortimer QC, described Mawdsley as: 'one of the most dangerous and determined killers held in this country'. He had already killed twice before the double murder in Wakefield Prison. Mawdsley had been transferred from Broadmoor Hospital to Wakefield Prison in March 1978. Within a few months he was fed up with Wakefield Prison and told another prisoner that he was thinking about 'doing someone in' as he would then be transferred to another prison. In a newspaper report several years later it was claimed that the day before the killings occurred Mawdsley's friend on the wing had been moved as Salney had reported him because he had been threatened by him.

On Friday 28 July, he had obtained a bladed weapon that was made from a piece of steel. From where or from whom he obtained the weapon was not known. The next day, before the exercise period, Salney Darwood, who is believed to have taught Mawdsley some French, had entered Mawdsley's cell. Mawdsley had then launched an attack on Salney with the weapon. He inflicted wounds to his head and neck, then using a ligature, garrotted him. He stuffed Salney's body under his bed then washed his hands. Tucking the knife into his waistband he went out to exercise. On his way back from exercise he passed William's cell and seeing that he was in he attacked him, stabbing him in the head, chest and stomach. He then concentrated his attack to William's head, bashing one side against the wall.

Mawdsley's counsel, Mr Edward Lyons QC said his client knew that he was a dangerous man and was very keen to have any treatment that was possible. His addiction to drugs such as LSD had gone. There appeared to be signs of improvement in his condition and there could be a time when he would not pose the danger that he currently did.

When Justice Cantley sentenced him to life he saw no reason to recommend a minimum period of detention as he thought that Mawdsley would never be released unless something happened that made it safe to release him. Justice Cantley said he was 'sorry for the prison service' having to deal with Mawdsley.

After sentencing, Mawdsley asked if he could say anything. Justice Cantley said: 'No, go away' and Mawdsley was escorted from the dock.

According to the *Yorkshire Post* on the 24 March 2000, in a letter published in a London newspaper (it did not specify which) on the previous day, Mawdsley asked for a cyanide pill so he could kill himself. In rejecting his plea, the Prison Service pointed out that all prisons including Wakefield operated an anti-suicide policy. He had claimed that he was buried alive in Wakefield Prison. A Prison Service spokesman said that every prisoner placed in high security prison had to complete a dispersal induction assessment before they could process through the prison system. As Mawdsley had failed to take part he remained where he was. In another letter, Mawdsley said he only killed rapists, paedophiles and sex offenders.

Mawdsley received more newspaper coverage the previous month than he had received for his various trials, because Charles Bronson (aka Michael Peterson) wanted to call Mawdsley as a witness during his trial for an incident that occurred in prison. His request was refused. It was reported that Mawdsley was being held in two cells under conditions similar to those in the film *Hannibal Lecter*.

Chapter 15

John Hope Dudgeon/Taylor

South Shields, 1979
Sheffield, 1988

In 1979, John Dudgeon was found guilty of manslaughter following his brutal killing of Vivien Scott, a nineteen-year-old, whom he had met at a South Shields nightclub. He served seventeen months of a four-year sentence. In November, he was in trouble again, violently attacking a young mother and her daughter, his new conviction resulting in serving four years of a seven-year term. Changing his name to Taylor, he moved back to South Shields and then to Sheffield where in 1989 he killed again.

1. South Shields, 1979
I just panicked

A Saturday afternoon 'kick about' is not unusual, plenty of boys enjoy a game of football on whatever ground is available. One such game was in progress at the back of the Veterans' Club, in Laygate, South Shields. The football flew over the railings so a ten-year-old boy went to retrieve it from Back Dacre Street. He saw a rolled up blanket under a carpet and, looking closer, he noticed a female body inside. The police soon had a possible name for the deceased: Vivien Scott, aged nineteen, who lived in Rembrandt Avenue, Whiteleas. She had been reported missing by her flat-mate Sandra Bartlett who had last seen Vivien on Thursday, 29 March when she left the flat with Elaine Pollard to go out for the night. Elaine left the *Tavern* nightclub at about 1.30 am and Vivien was talking to a man she had met at the club.

Vivien and Sandra had been due to appear before Hepburn magistrates on 2 April but Vivien had failed to appear. Sandra had then reported her missing. They were facing a charge of burglary. The victim was Vivien's mother and goods worth more than £1,000 had been stolen.

Detective Superintendent Gordon McMurchie led the investigation, with more than forty officers to assist him. It did not take long before the man she had been seen with in the nightclub was being questioned. He was interegated for forty hours and released without charge. Northumbria Police told reporters that a file had been sent to the Director of Public Prosecutions but they would not give any other information. The *Shields Gazette* reported that the case was notable for the amount of information not disclosed. On Sunday, the police would not disclose Vivien's name until the reporters had found out for themselves. On Tuesday, they would not reveal when Vivien had died nor would they disclose the cause of death, even though a post-mortem had been carried out by the Home Office pathologist, Dr Harvey McTaggart. The police refused to comment on claims that there had been a bag over her head and her feet were bound.

An inquest was opened by coroner Allan Henderson on 12 April. Dr McTaggart stated that Vivien died through asphyxia caused by suffocation and strangulation – not by natural causes. Her body had been found lying face down. Her feet were enclosed in a white plastic bag which had been secured by rope. Vivien's mother, Mrs Marie Scott, told the inquest that she had identified Vivien's body at 9 pm on Saturday. Detective Superintendent McMurchie said that a man had been questioned and a file sent to the Director of Public Prosecutions. The inquest was adjourned pending the outcome of further police enquiries.

On 30 April, Sandra Bartlett appeared before Hepburn magistrates and admitted breaking into Vivien's mother's house and stealing goods to a value of £1,113. All the stolen property except a ring was recovered. She was fined £50 with £10 costs – and ordered to pay £100 in compensation. The Director of Public Prosecution was still considering the file on Vivien's death.

On 8 May, John Hope Dudgeon, aged twenty-three, whose address was given as the Britannia public house, in Westoe Road,

South Shields, was accused of unlawfully killing Vivien and concealing her body. He was granted bail for the sum of £500, on condition that he continued to reside at the Britannia. On 14 May, he was found lying injured outside the pub. Police described the incident as 'domestic' and no further action was taken.

The case started at Newcastle Crown Court on Monday, 19 November 1979. Edward Lyons, for the prosecution, outlined his case. On the evening of 29 March, Vivien and Dudgeon had met at the *Tavern* night club. They left the club together and went to his bedsit in Laygate Lane. A few hours later Vivien was dead, having been suffocated and strangled. Dudgeon tried to conceal his responsibility for her death and he told a series of calculated lies to the police. In the prosecution view, they had gone to his bedsit and had had sex. Later on she got dressed and he engaged in some horseplay in an effort to persuade her to carry on the sexual activity. She had resisted and kicked him several times. He had then come behind her and put his right arm around her waist and then brought his left arm across her chest and up the side of her neck. Vivien had fallen forward on to the settee and he fell on top of her. He kept her in that position until she had stopped struggling, which was about six minutes. He had then stood up and she had fallen to the floor. When he had realised that Vivien was dead he rolled her into a blanket, tied it up, and then went to sleep. Later that morning, he carried her body down to the coalhouse. On the Sunday he moved her body to behind the Veterans' Club.

When Dudgeon was first questioned he denied any knowledge of Vivien but he soon changed his story and said that she had been in his room until about 4 am that morning but she had then left. In another version of events he said he had collapsed or fallen asleep and on coming around had found Vivien's body – but he soon changed that story as well. He had, therefore, given the police two statements. In the first Vivien had walked out of his bedsit. His second statement said they were both drunk and 'carrying on'.

Detective Chief Inspector Eric Sanderson told the jury about Dudgeon's various versions of events. When asked why he had not called for help, his reply was: 'I don't know, I was terrified, I just panicked.' He had waited until everyone had left the flats before he dragged Vivien's body downstairs and, finding a coalhouse open, put her there until he had time to think. On the Sunday night he moved her body to where it was found.

Dr Harvey McTaggart told the court that in his opinion considerable effort would have been needed to hold Vivien with her head buried in a settee. She would have lost consciousness within a minute but her heart would have continued beating for two to ten minutes, and during this time she could have recovered. The bruising and blood spots on her face and shoulders indicated that her death had been slow. Death was due to asphyxia, suffocation by external obstruction of the nose and mouth. Strangulation had occurred by pressure on the neck.

Kenneth Gray had a bedsit on the same floor as Dudgeon. They had both gone to do some decorating at the *Readhead Club* on 29 March. They had then gone to the *Miners' Hall* in Stanhope Road where they had about four pints of beer. They had then gone to *La Strada* but Dudgeon had then left to go to the *Tavern*. At 7 o'clock the next morning, Gray had gone to wake Dudgeon as he usually did but he was already up. Dudgeon had told

Sketch of John Didgeon. Carl Lawson

him he had had a girl in his room until 4 am but Kenneth had said she could not have left at that time because he had shown his girl to the door at the same time. Dudgeon made no reply to his comment. Dudgeon had come to his room several times after that night. He had stood on his chest of drawers and looked out of the window. From that position you could see the Veterans Club. When he saw police at the rear of the club he also saw a piece of carpet that had come from the bathroom.

Dudgeon went into the dock to give his version of the events. He said that he had been under the weather with drink that night. Later, he had met Vivien at the *Tavern* and she had come back to his bedsit. Once there they had had sex and later on they had had a 'slap and tickle' session. He had got hold of her from behind and she had fallen head-first onto the settee. He lay on top of her because he was exhausted after fooling around and due to the beer, so he had been trying to get his breath back. When he asked her if she had calmed down he got no reply so he stood up and she collapsed onto the floor. He had checked for signs of life and when he found none he felt bad. He tried to figure out what had happened and what to do next. He had then rolled her body into a blanket and secured it with rope. He fell asleep and when he woke he had thought about going to the police but could not bring himself to do it. His reason for moving the body, was so that it would be found.

He had tried to cover up his involvement in the hope that someone else would be charged. He had a job and, if his fiancé knew Vivien had been in his room, he felt that he would have lost his fiancé if he was charged. He had even suggested that her boyfriend might have killed her because of jealousy.

Dudgeon's counsel, Gerald Cole QC, said that his mistake was not seeking help when Vivien had died, if he had he would probably not even be on trial for manslaughter. Once he had made that mistake it was no surprise that he then lied to the police.

The jury of seven men and five women retired for nearly three hours before convicting him of manslaughter but acquitted him of obstructing the coroner. Justice McNeill said that it was quite clear that he had pressed her face into the settee for a significant period and that led to her death. Dudgeon was jailed for four years.

Dudgeon was released seventeen months later. In November 1982, he attacked and sexually assaulted a mother and her daughter. During the assault he stuck an eight inch knife into the mother and then tried suffocating her daughter with a pillow. The mother pulled the knife from her chest and went for him. He fled the scene. The judge decided that this convicted killer only deserved a seven year sentence for these offences. He was released four years later.

Changing his name to Taylor, he returned to South Shields. He went into a pub where a friend of Vivien worked. The friend did not believe Taylor's version of the events that led to her death and he was angry that Taylor was strutting around her home town. He told Taylor he was barred but Taylor refused to leave. In his own words he, 'let him have it'. Taylor suffered a broken cheekbone and reported the assault. In July 1987, Vivien's friend was sentenced to eighteen months for the attack on Taylor. Whilst he was serving his sentence at Durham Prison he heard that Taylor had killed again.

2. Sheffield, 1988

I just snapped

An ankle injury indirectly caused a death. John MacNamara owned the Moorcroft Snooker Hall in Sheffield but his painful ankle meant that he did not go to the club on the evening of Friday, 11 March 1988. His thirty-one-year-old attractive wife Susan ran the club that night but she was never to return home. The staff had left the club before midnight and Susan was alone counting the takings before locking up for the night. Susan's body was found sprawled in her Toyota Starlet car in the Upperthorpe area of Sheffield, her head was on the front seat and her legs on the rear seat and some of her clothing was missing. John went to the club to assist the police and he suggested her likely routine. When the roll from the electronic till was examined it showed that the evening's takings were £159. It also revealed that someone had been served a soft drink just after midnight, and there was another sale about an hour and a half later.

Robbery seemed a likely motive but the amount of violence used seemed to indicate otherwise. Susan's neck had been broken and she had been strangled.

The police started questioning club customers. They were asked if they had been in the club on the Friday night. If they replied 'yes' they were asked to name anyone else they had seen there and at what time. These questions resulted in John Taylor coming to the attention of the police. He was unemployed and had lived in lodgings opposite the club since January. As a club regular he was known to Susan and John. Looking into his record, the police soon found out that he was really John Dudgeon, having previous convictions included manslaughter, indecent assault and grievous bodily harm. His record and the violence used in the fatal assault on Susan made him the prime suspect. At first he denied killing Susan but after a while he claimed that he had snapped and squeezed her neck.

The case came to trial at Sheffield Crown Court in January 1989. The prosecution was presented by Martin Bethel QC. Taylor had arrived at the club around midnight and Susan had served him a soft drink as he was a regular. The till showed a second drink had been served at 1.36 am and a 'no sale' was registered at 1.43 am.

Taylor had told the police that as they walked to the door Susan had said something and he had snapped. He had wrapped his arm around her neck and squeezed. Taylor claimed that she had not struggled and things might have been different if she had. He had found her car keys then had driven around with Susan's body in the car before leaving it in Upperthorpe.

The pathologist, Professor Alan Usher told the court that Susan's face had been forced onto her chest, which resulted in her neck being broken. In his opinion her head had been held under her attacker's arm and her body swung around. She would have been paralysed and unable to defend herself. He could not say if she died in the club or her car. In reply to a question from Justice French, he said that the state of Susan's clothing pointed towards sexual interference but there was no other evidence to support a sexual assault.

Taylor decided to give evidence in his own defence. He had been out drinking with friends that evening and at the end of the night he left his friends and went to the snooker club. He claimed that Susan was very abrupt with a group of foreign students who came to the club for a game of snooker. He took her to task about it because the students' understanding of English was limited. Susan had said something in reply but he did not hear what she said and that annoyed him. He had grabbed Susan and she had fallen, pulling him down with her. As he fell he felt a pain in his chest because he had a broken rib. This angered him so he grabbed her by the neck and shook her. He heard her make a gurgling sound and realised that he had gone too far. He claimed that at no time did he have any intention of harming her.

On Friday, 20 January 1989, the jury convicted John Dudgeon (aka Taylor) of Susan's murder. He was sentenced to life with a tariff of twenty-five years but for some reason the Lord Chief Justice reduced it to sixteen years. The Home Secretary, Michael Howard, increased the sentence to twenty-five years. When his case was reviewed by the new Home Secretary, Jack Straw, he reduced it to twenty-two years. Dudgeon will be eligible to apply for parole in 2010.

Chapter 16

Paul Patrick Magee

Belfast, 1980
Tadcaster, 1992

In 1980, during the Troubles in Northern Ireland, Paul Patrick Magee, with others, was placed on trial following the killing of Captain Herbert Richard Westmacott of the Grenadier Guards and Stephen Magill, an RUC constable. The judge ruled that Magee was not guilty of Magill's killing but he was detained – with others – pending a decision regarding Westmacott. Using guns smuggled into Crumlin Road Prison, Magee and his IRA colleagues managed to escape. In their absence, Magee and four others were found guilty of Westmacott's murder. He was given a minimum sentence of twenty-five years, though it was not believed that he had fired a gun during Westmacott's murder. After Magee's escape he was arrested in Ireland and under the cross-border *Criminal Law Jurisdiction Act* sentenced to ten years, released in 1989. Granted bail in 1991, pending an extradition hearing relating to Westmacott's murder, Magee ignored restrictions and fled to England. In 1992, at Tadcaster, he fatally shot a young special constable, Glenn Goodman, for which he received a minimum term sentence of thirty years. In 1998, Magee was transferred to Port Laoise Prison in Ireland but was subsequently freed under the terms of the Good Friday Agreement.

1. Belfast, 1980

Take good care of it

During the troubles in Northern Ireland the IRA were known to phone the security services claiming that suspicious activity had been seen at a house. They hoped to lure them into a well prepared ambush. The security services knew that some calls might be genuine so they had to respond to most calls with caution.

On the afternoon of Friday, 2 May 1980, an eight-man Special Air Service Patrol were dressed in civilian clothes. They were in two cars, three men in one and five men including their officer, Captain Herbert Richard Westmacott, were in a Morris Marina. Just before two o'clock they received a call that there was suspicious activity at a house in Antrim Road, north Belfast. As the patrol got near to the address they slipped on fluorescent-coloured armbands to identify themselves as security forces so other security forces did not shoot at them if they came across the incident. In Antrim Road, Captain Westmacott's car drove up to the house where suspicious activity had been reported. The other car turned down a side street so that the rear of the houses were covered.

The four men with Capt Westmacott rapidly deployed from their car and took up covering positions. As they did this they came under heavy automatic high-velocity fire from an upstairs window of one of the houses. The driver of the SAS team used the car as cover and returned fire, using his sub-machine gun, as the other men ran to a doorway. Capt Westmacott was the last to exit the vehicle as he had been sat in the middle of the back seat. He did not get far before he was shot in his shoulder and head. Westmacott fell, fatally wounded, about six feet from the doorway. Whilst one of the three men who made it to the doorway provided cover, the other two checked the house but found it was empty. Realising that they had searched the wrong house they then took up covering positions against the next door house. The team in the second car had detained a man who was heading towards a Ford Transit van parked behind the house in Antrim Road.

The IRA men could not escape, four SAS men covered the front of the house and another team covered the rear. One of the SAS men shouted to the gunmen to throw out their weapons and come out with their hands in the air. The gunmen replied that they would not come out until the RUC arrived. Then they said that they had an M60 machine gun and threw a bullet case out to prove it. When challenged again to come out they claimed to have a woman with them. RUC and uniformed soldiers had quickly formed a cordon around the area. The SAS team then received a radio message telling them to withdraw from the area. They got back into their shot-up car with its flat tyres and reversed it to the junction with Limestone Road where they left it. They were then picked up and returned to their base.

At 2.10 pm, a Lieutenant-Colonel of the Royal Artillery Field Regiment questioned the gunman who had been detained by the SAS team at the rear of the house. He was being held in an Army Land Rover and the Lieutenant-Colonel asked him how many men were in the house but he refused to answer. When it was suggested that there might be three men in the house he said that this figure could be right.

RUC Superintendent Charles Morrison took over negotiations to get the gunmen to surrender themselves and their weapons. He used a loud hailer to talk to the gunmen who were in the first floor room. One of the men had come to the window and asked for a priest to be involved in their negotiations. After a priest arrived, the negotiations resumed and Superintendent Morrison guaranteed their safety. A man at the window turned towards the broken window with a white cloth stuck on the end of a rifle and placed in on the ledge outside the window. He turned again, then placed another rifle on the ledge. He then lowered an M60 machine gun, with its ammunition belt still in place, onto the window ledge saying as he did so 'take good care of it'.

A little later, three men emerged from the house and walked towards the waiting RUC officers. They were identified as Angelo Fusco, aged twenty-three of Slieveban Drive, Joseph Patrick Thomas Doherty, aged twenty-seven of Spamount Street and Robert Joseph Campbell, aged twenty-six of Ballymurphy Crescent, all of Belfast. Joseph Doherty and Angelo Fusco had given raised clenched fist salutes and shouts in support of the Provos as they left the house. The man detained at the rear of the house was Paul Patrick Magee, aged thirty-two of Glenalina Gardens, Belfast. The incident was not reported in the *Belfast Telegraph* as its journalists were on strike at the time. Captain Westmacott left a widow, Victoria and a six-month-old daughter, Honor. In the *London Gazette* dated 20 October 1980, it was announced that Captain Herbert Richard Wesmacott of the

Grenadier Guards was posthumously awarded the Military Cross.

The M60 machine gun was of special interest to the RUC. On Wednesday 9 April, one had been used in the murder of William Stephen Magill, a twenty-four-year-old RUC constable. He had been in an RUC Land Rover patrol that had been sent to investigate a burglary at Suffolk Library in west Belfast. The librarian had reported the burglary at 8.30 that morning. As the patrol turned up at 9 o'clock, IRA gunmen hiding in a house that they had taken over in Doon Road, opened fire on them. Constable William Stephen Magill was fatally wounded and two other officers were seriously wounded.

The ambush on the RUC patrol led to another murder on Friday, 25 April. The IRA thought that Michael Madden, a sixty-eight-year-old retired civil servant, who had worked for the Ministry of Agriculture, had given the RUC information about the ambush. Michael lived alone in Lenadoon Avenue and two IRA gunmen went to his home. They took him into the back garden and shot him six times. In January 1981, an inquest into his death was held, an RUC Detective Inspector said that there was no truth in the claim that he had provided information about the ambush. His murder remains unsolved.

The men came to trial at Belfast Crown Court on Monday, 27 April 1981. It was a trial without a jury. Mr Justice Hutton would hear the evidence then decide on a verdict for each person and each charge. There were thirteen men in the dock, with charges ranging from murder to membership of the IRA. An application was made to adjourn the trial for a week as defence lawyers had only received extra evidence a week before the Easter recess. One of the defence lawyers also said that he had only seen the full indictment which contained thirty-six counts at 10 o'clock that morning. Justice Hutton refused the request for the week's ajournment but granted a few hours for the indictments to be examined. The event was reported as the 'M60 Trial'.

The men charged with the murder of Captain Herbert Richard Westmacott were Angelo Fusco, Joseph Campbell, Joseph Doherty and Paul Magee. Those charged with the murder of Constable William Stephen Magill were Angelo Fusco, Paul Magee, Emmanuel Fusco, aged twenty-three of Sileveban Drive, Anthony Gerard Sloan,

Crumlin Road Courthouse. The Author

aged twenty-six of Summerville Drive and Michael Anthony McKee, aged twenty-four of New Barnsley Crescent, all in Belfast.

After a few weeks, Emmanuel Fusco pleaded guilty to the manslaughter of Constable Magill and was removed from the dock to await sentencing at the end of the trial. A month into the trial, on Thursday, 28 May, three of the men on lesser charges were granted separate trials – one was remanded into custody pending the new trial and the other two men were granted bail. In the afternoon, Justice Hutton ruled that Paul Patrick Magee and Michael Anthony McKee should have a verdict of not guilty recorded against them with regard to the murder of Constable Magill. He ruled that it was possible McKee had not been involved in the shooting of Constable Magill but he had helped with the disposal of the weapons a few hours afterwards. Justice Hutton ruled that Magee's participation in Captain Herbert Richard Westmacott murder could not be used by the Crown to strengthen their case against him with regard to the killing of Constable Magill.

A major development occurred on the afternoon of Wednesday, 10 June. At about 4 o'clock, seven of the men on trial for the murder offences were having meetings with their legal representatives in the legal visit area of Crumlin Road Prison. The IRA men, using guns that had been smuggled into the prison at some point, threatened the solicitors and ten warders. Ordering them all to keep quite, the IRA men told two of the warders to strip off their uniforms. Joined by another inmate and a few warders as hostages, the seven IRA men then split into two groups. With two of them acting as warders they made for the main gate. Alerted to the escape, a squad of about eighteen warders armed with batons attempted to block their exit but had to back off when the IRA men opened fire. On getting through the front gate, the first group got into a get-away car and escaped. Armed police and soldiers challenged the second group and a running gun battle developed, but in the confusion the IRA men escaped.

Sketch-map showing Crumlin Road Prison, Court and Hospital. The Author

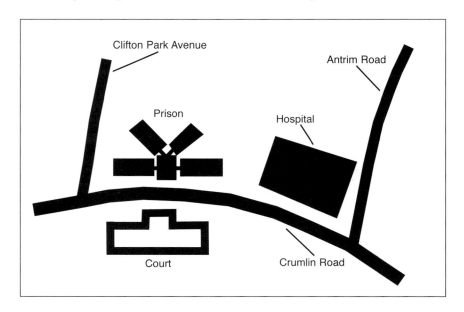

On Friday, 12 June, the deputy governor of Crumlin Road Prison confirmed to Justice Hutton that the prisoners had escaped from custody. Justice Hutton decided to give his verdict on them in their absence. In relation to the murder charges he gave the following verdicts: Angelo Fusco, Robert Joseph Campbell, Paul Patrick Magee and Joseph Patrick Thomas Doherty were all found guilty of Captain Westmacott's murder. Angelo Fusco and Anthony Gerard Sloan were acquitted of the murder of Constable Magill.

Before passing sentence, Justice Hutton, told counsel representing the escaped men that as they had voluntarily absented themselves from the court they had given up their entitlement to being represented by their counsel in mitigation. He sentenced Fusco, Campbell and Doherty to a minimum of thirty years. Justice Hutton said that he believed Magee had not fired a gun during Captain Westmacott's murder but he was one of the gang so he sentenced him to a minimum of twenty-five years. As Magee was at liberty he was, as we shall see, free to kill again, this time in Yorkshire, in 1992.

2. Tadcaster, 1992
Their answers didn't satisfy the officers

On the night of Saturday, 6 June 1992, Glenn Thomas Goodman, a thirty -seven-year-old lorry driver, had left his wife Fiona and eleven-month-old son Tom at home. Three weeks earlier, he had been sworn in as a special constable with the North Yorkshire Police Force. On Monday he was due to have an interview with Cleveland Police as he wished to become a full-time police officer. That Saturday night was to be his first night patrol. He accompanied PC Alexander 'Sandy' Kelly as they drove around the Tadcaster area. Earlier that evening, there had been a bomb incident at the Royal Festival Hall in London. Around 3 o'clock on Sunday morning, they saw a red Ford Sierra car parked near a slip road from the A64 near Tadcaster. As they got closer the car drove away and they followed it, then flagged it down at Headley Bar, near Sutton.

The officers approached the car to speak to the driver. The driver

SPC Glenn Thomas Goodman with his son, Tom. With kind permission of Glenn's widow

and his passenger spoke with Irish accents and the earlier bomb incident made the police officers very wary. The driver gave his name as Ryan and was asked to sit in the police car whilst a form to produce his driving documents was filled in. He was given the form and returned to his car. Neither the driver nor passenger could give a convincing account of their movements. PC Kelly returned to the patrol car to check on a licence produced by Ryan. The radio check indicated that the licence could be stolen. PC Kelly then requested assistance. Whilst PC Kelly made the request, SPC Glenn Goodman stood between the two cars. The driver got out of the Sierra and walked towards SPC Goodman, as he got close to Glenn he brought his hands up and Sandy saw a hand gun. The driver shot Glenn twice in the chest then shot at Sandy through the windscreen of the patrol car . One bullet hit Sandy in the chest the other missed him and hit the steering wheel. Sandy flung himself across the passenger seat and shouted: 'Ten nine! Ten nine!' (the code for immediate assistance required by an officer) into the radio. The driver then walked over to the patrol car and, using another hand gun, shot Sandy at close range. One of the bullets aimed at his head, but hit the radio he was using to summon help. Returning to the Sierra the gunman and his passenger drove off at speed.

As others raced to the scene an alert was put out to all officers about the shooting incident. PCs Susan Larkin and Mark Whitehouse were questioning another motorist when they heard the alert. They then saw a car approaching at speed. Leaving the motorist they had stopped, they set off in pursuit. As the red Ford Sierra approached the village of Burton Salmon, nine miles south of Tadcaster, it stopped and the passenger got out. He had a gun, later identified as a Kalashnikov automatic rifle, and pointed it towards the police car. PC Whitehouse put the car in reverse as the gunman opened fire, the windscreen shattered, but both officer occupants escaped injury. The gunman continued to advance on the patrol car, which had got stuck on a fence when it had reversed, when headlights were seen approaching. Returning to the Sierra, the gunman and driver made good their escape. The approaching car that had scared off the gunmen was not a police vehicle, but was the motorist that PCs Larkin and Whitehouse had stopped before setting off in pursuit of the Sierra. About twenty minutes later, a burning car was spotted in a field, it was the red Sierra.

Glenn and Sandy were rushed to St James Hospital in Leeds, Glenn dying on the operating table shortly after arrival. Sandy had been shot in the chest, arm and buttocks but, following treatment, he was described as stable despite a bullet being left in him. Following questioning of the police officers, descriptions of the two suspects were released. Both were white and spoke with Irish accents. The driver was about twenty-eight-years-old, 5ft 8ins in height of medium build, with mousy-coloured hair and moustache. He was wearing round, metal-rimmed glasses, grey or blue jeans, blue and white hooped sweat shirt and white trainers. He wore a gold ring on his wedding finger. The passenger was clean shaven, aged in his mid-forties, 5ft 8ins tall with short grey hair, receding at the front. He was wearing a grey lounge suit, blue and white stripped shirt, blue tie and white trainers.

The car had been set alight near the A1 close to the M62. The A1 ran north to south and the M62 ran east to west. The A1 joined the M62 at junction 33 and westwards at junction 29 the M62 joined the M1. If the gunmen could get another vehicle they could easily head north to Scotland, south to London, west to Manchester or east to Hull. Reports of stolen vehicles in the area received more attention than was usually given to them. Police searches in the local area failed to find the gunmen. There were concerns that the men might have an arms dump or safe house in the area. The two hand guns and Kalashnikov suggested that the gunmen could have been a close-quarter assassination squad who had been targeting someone in the Yorkshire area.

Pontefract lies just south of the M62, it is about five miles from Burton Salmon and it was here that the gunmen were arrested four days later. They were each arrested separately as they tried to buy a fresh change of clothes in the town. Their appearance and accent caused the shop's staff concern and they rang the police, an officer saw him and followed. Whilst awaiting back up, he resisted arrest. When the driver went into Pontefract a few hours later, he did not resist when arrested. The state of their clothing suggested that they had been hiding out in the countryside and not in a safe house. Later, enquiries indicated that they knew the area quite well as they had hidden in a culvert, under a main road, near to the Heron Service Station on the A1 near Knottingley, in order to escape the searching police. The Kalashnikov was discovered in a ditch near to Pontefract but the two hand guns were never found.

Although the murder of Glenn Thomas Goodman had occurred in Yorkshire it was at Bow Street Magistrates Court in London that the gunmen were charged. They were Paul Patrick Magee, an unemployed forty-two-year-old from Belfast and Michael O'Brien, a twenty-seven-year-old Irish national.

The case came to court on Monday, 15 March 1993 at the Old Bailey, with Mr Justice Laws presiding. John Nutting QC, outlined the prosecution case. The two men were both charged with the murder of SPC Glenn Thomas Goodman, the attempted murders of PCs Alexander 'Sandy' Kelly, Susan Larkin and Mark Whitehouse and possession of a firearm. A palm print of Magee's was found on the door of Glenn and Sandy's police car. A fragment of a police document given to O'Brien at the traffic stop was found in his clothing when he was arrested and forensics linked them to the Kalashnikov. O'Brien admitted having been the driver but denied firing any shots.

The trial lasted eleven days and on Monday, 29 March, after seven hours deliberations, the jury reached unanimous verdicts. They found Paul 'Dingus' Magee guilty of the murder of SPC Glenn Thomas Goodman and the attempted murder of the three PCs. Michael O'Brien was acquitted of the murder of Glenn Goodman and the attempted murder of Sandy Kelly but convicted of the attempted murder of PCs Susan Larkin and Mark Whitehouse. Both were also convicted of possessing a firearm with intent to endanger life.

During the trial the IRA were not mentioned nor was the prosecution able to say why the men were in the area that night. No trace of where they were operating from was found. Their Sierra had been damaged by another vehicle whilst it was parked in a west London a week before the murder. The next day, Justice Laws sentenced Magee to life with a minimum term of thirty years for the murder of Glenn. He was given life for the attempted murders of the PCs with a minimum term of twenty-five years for each offence and fifteen years for possessing firearms with intent to endanger life. Before sentencing, O'Brien's counsel, Michael Mansfield QC told the court that O'Brien was appalled by what had happened but he was still sentenced to eighteen years for the attempted murders of PC' Larkin and Whitehouse and ten years for the firearms offence.

After Magee's escape from Crumlin Road Prison in 1981 he had gone to Ireland. He was arrested in Tralee and under the cross-border Criminal Law Jurisdiction Act was sentenced to ten years for escaping from prison, but released in 1989. In 1991, he had been granted bail pending the outcome of a hearing into an extradition application from Northern Ireland to serve his sentence for the murder of Captain Herbert Richard Westmacott. He jumped bail and headed for England. Justice Laws asked which court had granted him bail and was told that it was the Irish Supreme Court. On 5 May 1998, Magee was transferred to Port Laoise Prison in Eire. Under the terms of the Good Friday Agreement he is now free.

There is a memorial to Glenn Goodman at the junction of Wetherby Road and Station Road in Tadcaster.

Chapter 17

Keith John Ward

Bradford, 1983
Birkinshaw, 1989

Julie Stead was strangled to death by Keith Ward, the culmination of a tempestuous relationship, in 1983. Due to an accepted 'provocation' plea, he was jailed for just four years. Later, Ward was given a two-year custodial sentence for assaulting his girlfriend, Valerie Middleton. Whilst on prison leave, in 1989, he returned to Valerie and killed her when she was taking a bath. For this second killing he received a life sentence with no recommendation for a minimum term.

1. Bradford, 1983
He could not remember killing her

The obituary notice in the Bradford *Telegraph and Argus* on Saturday 12 March 1983 said that Julie Stead had 'died suddenly'.

Julie Stead had been found dead in her home in Hopbine Avenue, West Bowling, Bradford on Tuesday, 8 March 1983. Her nine-year-old daughter discovered her mother's body in her bedroom. Next to the bed was a cot in which lay, unharmed, another child. The police did not need to do much investigating to identify Julie's killer. He had handed himself in to the police.

The previous night, twenty-five-year-old Julie had attempted a reconciliation with Keith Ward. They had separated because of his violent behaviour. Julie had met him in 1981 when she worked in a pub in Bradford. They had an on-off relationship for two years, she even went into a hostel at one point to avoid him. The welfare workers put her into a safe house but he found her. When she was

Hopbine Avenue. The Author

pregnant he punched her and she went into premature labour. He had been telling Julie that he was divorcing his wife but when she found out that his wife was pregnant, their relationship deteriorated even more. For some reason Julie decided to give it another chance so she met him on Monday, 7 March. The following morning, as the two eldest children were downstairs getting ready for school, Ward strangled Julie. Twenty-six-year-old Keith John Ward of Avenue Road, West Bowling, Bradford was charged by the police with the murder of Julie Stead.

Ward came to trial at Leeds Crown Court in early December 1983. The proceedings lasted three days. Police Sergeant David Cash said that the relationship had been stormy from the start, with various beatings. It was plain that Ward was a violent man. Ward's version of what happened that Tuesday morning was that Julie had provoked him by saying he was not the father of their child, that he could not remember strangling her as he had blacked out; and he had not realised that Julie was dead.

The jury seems to have accepted Ward's version of events as they acquitted him of murder and convicted him of 'manslaughter due to provocation'. Justice McCullough said that the provocation was by no means the gravest, and then sentenced Ward to a just four years. The sentence did not go down well locally as that same week a Bradford burglar was sentenced to nine years.

On Friday, 9 December, the Bradford *Telegraph and Argus* carried a report that West Yorkshire Police denied withholding evidence. Ward had been subject to an injunction banning him from seeing Julie for several months leading up to her death. The jury were not told about the this. Detective Chief Superintendent Trevor Lapish said that the decision not to include the information was taken by the court – not the police.

Julie had frequently reported Ward to the police for assault but the police regarded her complaints as 'domestic' so they failed to take any action against Ward. They also failed to act when Julie reported a burglary at her home that she suspected Ward had committed. After strong local protests concerning the police handling of the case an officer from another force looked into the complaints. As a result of his inquiry, three officers were warned about their conduct in failing to record or take certain actions. In June 1985, Sir Michael Havers, the Attorney General, admitted that he was unhappy with the handling of the inquiry and that the Director of Public Prosecutions had been sorely misled by the officers involved in the case.

Ward's next victim knew he had killed Julie and the police obtained a conviction for Ward assaulting her (for which he was sentenced to two years). As we shall see, he killed his second victim on prison leave whilst serving the sentence.

2. Birkenshaw, 1989
She didn't make it plain it was over

Following a phone call at six-fifty pm on Monday, 13 March 1989, police went to a council house in Albert Way, Birkenshaw. The call had been from a man who claimed he had killed his wife. When the police arrived they found a woman's body in the bath. Her

Albert Way, Birkenshaw, Bradford. D Speight

bloodstained head had been battered. Dr Michael Green, a pathologist, was called to the scene and after he had made his initial examination the woman's body was removed to the mortuary. The post-mortem showed that she had been struck around the head, and that the weapon was estimated to weigh about six pounds.

The police soon had the outline of the case. The victim was Mrs Valerie Middleton, a thirty-year-old divorcee with two children. She had been killed in her own home by her boyfriend, Keith John Ward, the man who had called the police to the scene. Ward was on leave from Lindholme Prison as he was due for release in the September. He was in prison because in 1988 he had attacked Valerie. He had punched her about the head, injuring an eye and breaking her nose, so that she needed stitches to the wounds. In February 1989 the probation service had asked Valerie if she would have him at her home when he had a weekend leave the following month. She had said she would.

Ward had spent the weekend with Valerie and had gone to the *Golden Fleece* pub on the Monday. He told a barmaid, who knew the couple, that Valerie would not give him an answer as to whether he could move back in with her when he finished his sentence. Instead of returning to Lindholme Prison, he went back to Valerie's. Whilst she was having a bath an argument developed and Ward battered her about the head. He also told the police that Valerie had persuaded him into a suicide pact but he soon dropped that version.

In February 1990, Ward's case came to trial at Leeds Crown Court before Justice French. His plea of guilty to manslaughter was not accepted by the prosecution who wanted him indicted for murder. Mr Christopher Holland QC, said that the provocation claim Ward made did not stand up to scrutiny. A naked woman in a bath with her back to the door was unlikely to provoke a man, who had previously seriously injured her, by telling him about affairs with other men. Her death was due to seven blows to the back of her head and one to her forehead. The weapon used had not been found.

Ward went into the dock to give his version of events. He had killed Valerie but he could not recall doing it. He had known her for eleven years and had lived with her for the last three years. On the Monday, Valerie had not wanted him to return to prison. He had left her to return to prison but called into the pub and whilst there he decided to go back to her. He was running her a bath when she found another woman's name on a piece of paper in his jacket. She had then begun taunting him about her sexual experiences with other men. He had struck her with something, but he could only remember coming to in the bedroom.

Christopher Holland cross-examined Ward and said: 'Isn't this the key to the problem, that as soon as she made it clear the relationship was over, you were too jealous to let her live?' Ward's response was: 'She didn't make it plain it was over. I didn't read it as such. She was just annoyed.'

Maybe the jury thought that his failure to say what the weapon was, was an indication that the attack was premeditated. He must have hidden it before he called the police as it had not been found.

It only took the jury forty-five minutes to reject his provocation plea and find him guilty of murder. Justice French sentenced Ward to life but made no recommendation for a minimum sentence. The jury then heard that in December 1983 he had stood trial for the murder of his girlfriend, Julie Stead, who had been strangled at her Bradford home in March 1982. That jury had accepted his plea of provocation and convicted him of manslaughter, so he was sentenced to four years.

Valerie had known that Ward had killed before. Julie Stead's family had contacted Leeds Women's Aid to warn them about Ward and they had written to Valerie to warn her. Whilst he was in prison for the assault on her, Valerie had started seeing another man and was due to start a new job. She had once told a friend she feared that one day he would kill her.

Chapter 18

George Stuart Naylor

Bradford, 1985 and 1995

This case relates to the killing of two women in the Bradford area by a man who had a string of previous convictions, including the rape of an elderly lady. Released from prison in 1993 after a manslaughter charge for the killing of Deborah Kershaw, George Naylor went on to kill again, his victim being eighteen-year-old prostitute, Maureen Stepan. Despite a second trial and appeals, Naylor's life sentence was confirmed in 2006.

1. Bradford, 1985

...no money to pay her...

At ten to one on the morning of Tuesday, 17 December 1985, a police Ford Transit van was on patrol in the City Road area of Bradford when the officers in it noticed a suspicious Vauxhall Viva car. They decided to question the driver but he would not stop so they chased him. At about one o'clock, the driver of the car stopped near the entrance to the Norman Arch at the entrance to Lister Park, Manningham Lane, Bradford. He got out of the Viva and ran off, pursued by the officers from the van. They soon caught him and then realised that he was not a Christmas thief – what the officers were really looking for in the run up to the festive season. The driver appeared to be a killer since a woman's body was found in the vehicle.

The forty-one-year old male driver was arrested and taken to the police station for questioning. Detective Inspector John Gamble was put in charge of the investigation. That day's edition of the Bradford *Telegraph and Argus* carried an appeal by DI Gamble for

Norman Arch, Manningham Lane, Bradford. D Speight

anyone to contact him who had seen the Viva in City Road, Bilton Place or Lower Globe Street areas around twenty to one that morning.

The next day, George Stuart Naylor, aged forty-one, of Roundhill Street, West Bowling appeared before the city's magistrates charged with the murder of Miss Deborah Kershaw, aged twenty-two who lived in the Allerton area of Bradford. Naylor's solicitor, Mr Stephen Couch asked for reporting restrictions to be lifted, as he said that the appropriate charge was one of manslaughter not murder. He also praised the professionalism of the police officers and DI John Gamble, thanking them for the assistance they had provided.

At Leeds Crown Court on Wednesday, 26 November 1986, Naylor was convicted of the manslaughter of Deborah. Naylor had told the court that he had picked Deborah up in Lumb Lane and they had gone to a side street for sex. He claimed that when he told her he had no money to pay her she attacked him and he had strangled her as he defended himself. He had been driving around with her body in his Viva, wondering what to do, when he saw the police Transit van and fled in a panic. The jury decided that the provocation reduced the charge from murder to manslaughter.

Justice Turner sentenced Naylor to life because he was aware of Naylor's previous convictions. After convicting him the jury was told that, in October 1985, just eight weeks before he killed Deborah, he had been released after serving ten years of a fifteen year sentence for raping a sixty-year-old spinster who lived in the same block of flats in Manchester Road, Bradford. According to a report years later, in the *Telegraph and Argus* (Friday, 2 February 1997) Naylor was convicted of armed robbery when he was aged seventeen in 1962, possessing an offensive weapon in 1963, assault in 1966 and 1971, criminal damage and assault on a police officer in 1972; and theft in 1973 and 1974. In May 1975 he had been convicted of burglary for which he was finally sent to prison, for a short sentence. In was in December 1975 that Naylor raped the spinster. If the jury had been aware of his convictions they might had decided it was murder not manslaughter.

Naylor felt aggrieved that he had been sentenced to life when he had been convicted of manslaughter so he appealed against his sentence. In July 1987, Lord Justice Watkins ruled that the medical evidence showing that Naylor was a danger to the public was 'barren'. Why Justice Watkins was bothered about the medical evidence when Naylor's criminal history clearly showed he was a danger to the public is not clear. Justice Watkins decided that a man who had already been sentenced to fifteen years for rape and burglary only deserved eleven years for manslaughter. This meant that Naylor was released in 1993 and, as we shall see, was free to kill another Bradford woman, Maureen Stepan, in 1995. If Justice Watkins had not quashed the life sentence that Justice Turner had imposed on Naylor, then Maureen would not have been killed. When Naylor was on trial in 1997 for his second killing the *Crime (Sentences) Act* was making it way through Parliament. The act means that anyone convicted of a second serious violent or sexual assault now gets an automatic life sentence.

2. Bradford, 1995
I will be out within a year

At eight o'clock on the night of Friday 9 June 1995, Talat Khan called at Maureen Stepan's back-to-back home in Washington Street, Girlington, Bradford. Entering the lounge, he saw Maureen's naked body laid out on the floor. Mr Khan called for the police but the investigation was hindered at the beginning as police resources were soon stretched. The Manningham area of Bradford is about a mile from Girlington and, an hour and a half after Maureen's body was found, the arrest of two youths led to a serious breakdown in public order. Further arrests were made when more officers arrived. A crowd of sixty marched to the nearby Lawcroft House police station in Lilycroft Road to demand the release of the arrested youths. The police arrested six more youths and a crowd of around 300 gathered in Oak Lane. Pallets were placed in the road and set alight and the disorder spread. This situation led to more than a hundred police officers being drafted in from surrounding West Riding towns to help restore public order. The pathologist was delayed getting to Washington Street until later on the Saturday morning.

St Philips and Washington Street, Girlington, Bradford. D Speight

Detective Superintendent Malcolm Mawson said that Maureen Stepan was an eigthteen-year-old prostitute, five foot six inches tall, of slim build with blonde shoulder-length hair, who had a drug problem. She used to take clients back to her home. He asked anyone who saw Maureen between midnight and eight o'clock on the Friday night to contact the police. The back door to her home had been open but it had been damaged during a recent burglary and had not yet been properly repaired. Enquiries by his officers revealed that a neighbour, Nazim Akhtar, had been woken up by screams coming from Maureen's house, at three o'clock that morning. He did not regard the incident as serious as he often heard screams and the sound of fighting coming from the property.

Within a week the police had a prime suspect. George Stuart Naylor, a fifty-one-year-old scrap metal man came to their attention for various little reasons and a major one. He had left the area within days of the murder and returned to Newcastle.

Previously, Naylor had returned to his bed-sit in Alva Terrace, Shipley an hour after screams were heard coming from Maureen's home. When he got home he had washed his clothes. On the Saturday he was seen cleaning his car on several occasions. In the early hours of Sunday morning he had been arrested for stealing newspapers. As we have seen, he had also killed Deborah Kershaw, another Bradford prostitute, ten years earlier. For that he had been sentenced to eleven years, after an appeal. Following questioning he was charged with murdering Maureen.

In January 1997, the jury at Sheffield Crown Court were told about Naylor's previous conviction for the manslaughter of Deborah Kershaw, even then his trial was to last four weeks. Paul Worsley QC, prosecuted the case, he told the jury that Maureen was killed because Naylor's wife, Linda, had thrown him out of the family home because of his violent behaviour. He had then moved back to the West Riding and got a bedsit in Shipley. Working as a scrap metal man provided him with the money to pay for keeping his car on the road and going drinking in Bradford. On the evening of Thursday, 8 June, he had phoned Linda on several occasions but she refused to take the calls. He then brooded in the *Raging Bull* pub, Thornton Road, Bradford.

At twenty to three that Friday morning Naylor was in Westgate, Bradford and, seeing a public phone booth, had called Linda but, again, she would not take the call. He then drove to the Listerhills area where Maureen had just turned up to look for clients. She got into his car and directed him to her home. Within twenty minutes of picking her up Naylor was strangling her with her own tights. He had then abused her body with a lighted cigarette and placed the ash in various places. He returned to his bedsit and washed all the clothes he had been wearing that night. Having cleaned his car he dropped those clothes at a relative's in Bradford before setting off to Newcastle.

Forensic examination of these clothes at the Home Office Forensic Laboratory revealed microscopic specks of blood on the knee of his jeans. Testing the blood showed that it was a 1 in 14,000 chance that the blood was not Maureen's. When Naylor gave evidence he explained that he had picked up Maureen earlier that night and had paid her £15 for sex in his car before dropping her off near to where he had picked her up.

It took the jury two days to reach a 11-1 majority verdict on the murder charge. They returned their verdict on Thursday, 6 February 1997. They then learnt that as well as the manslaughter conviction Naylor had a string of convictions dating back to 1962, including armed robbery, assault, burglary, assaulting a police officer and rape. Justice Blofeld then sentenced him to life with a twenty year minimum tariff. Before leaving the dock, Naylor called out that he would be out in a year. He appealed against his conviction on the grounds that the jury had been told about his manslaughter conviction.

On Thursday, 30 April 1998, Naylor's appeal started at the Court of Appeal (Criminal Division). The judges were Lord Justice Roch, Justice Sachs and Justice Collins. The next day they allowed the appeal and granted Naylor a retrial. They said they would give their reasons in due course. They then had discussions, with Mr J Stewart QC, representing Naylor and Mr P F Worsley QC, for the Crown, concerning the location of the retrial. There had been too much publicity of the trial in Leeds and Bradford, Naylor came from Newcastle so that caused problems if the trial was held there. Manchester was another possibility and even London was considered. The appeal judges decided that the retrial should be held in Sheffield but Mr Stewart could request a change if he so wished. Mr Stewart made no application for bail and Lord Justice Roch directed that Naylor remain in custody pending retrial.

The second trial started in January 1999 at Sheffield Crown Court with Justice Ebsworth presiding. The jury were not made aware of his previous manslaughter conviction. Mr Paul Worsley prosecuted the case again. On Monday, 1 February, the six-man, six-woman jury returned a 10-2 majority guilty verdict on the murder charge. Three of the woman jurors wept when they were told about Naylor's previous convictions and the first trial. Sentencing him to life with a twenty-year minimum tariff, Justice Ebsworth told him: 'What you did to her was pick her up from the streets, you killed her and you then degraded her body using it in a way that can only be described as using it as if it was an ashtray. That in my judgment clearly arose from the desire to show contempt and anger for women.'

Naylor appealed again and in December 1999 he was granted leave to appeal. At the end of April 2001 he went on hunger strike in Durham Prison in protest at delays in getting documents for his latest appeal. Legal wrangles and Naylor's demands for trial transcripts meant that the appeal was not heard until May 2004.

On 5 May, the three judges at the Criminal Appeal Court decided that his conviction was safe and rejected his appeal. Lord Justice Pill said that the case against Naylor had been powerful and the circumstantial evidence had been strong. Naylor had claimed that he had picked up a prostitute, who was probably Maureen, at quarter-past one that morning and they had then parted. At the trial a man claimed to have been with Mauren from half-past twelve until nearly three o'clock – which meant Naylor's account of picking her up at quarter past one was suspect – if correct.

The main grounds for the appeal had been that Justice Ebsworth had misdirected the jury on issues arising from the evidence of a barman. He described a customer coming into the *Raging Bull* pub twice on the fateful night. The first time was from a quarter to eleven until eleven, then from half-past twelve until ten-past two. Some of his description fitted Naylor but other aspects of it had not. Lord Justice Pill said that there was not doubt that Naylor had been to the pub at least once that night. He acknowledged that Justice Ebsworth could have put the issue to the jury more clearly but he concluded that the jury had not been misled.

On Tuesday, 14 February 2006, Justice Owen had the task of setting his minimum tariff under the *Criminal Justice Act 2003* (the Home Secretary was no longer entitled to alter a tariff set by the trial judge). In her report to the Home Secretary, Justice Ebsworth had recommended a minimum term of twenty years, the Lord Chief Justice had agreed with her, stating that a long punitive term was plainly merited.

Justice Owen also concluded that a twenty-year minimum tariff was required. In his final paragraph he made it plain that for the protection of the public Naylor would continue to be detained after the tariff had expired.

Chapter 19

David Simmonds

Beverley, 1988
Lincoln, 1999

Davidd Simmonds killed his estranged wife, Gillian in 1988, drowning her in the bath during a fit of jealousy – and then attempted suicide. Released from prison on licence, he had begun an affair with a Lincoln art gallery worker, Janet Richards who became increasingly concerned about his apparently possessive nature. Rejected, Simmonds strangled Janet and committed suicide.

1. Beverley, 1988
She went back to her first husband

Gillian Simmonds, aged thirty-nine, had left her second husband, forty-one-year-old David Simmonds and then moved in with her previous mother-in-law. She and her first husband, Alfred Spinks had kept in touch since their divorce sixteen years ago. They had met again at a family funeral in 1987 (according to a report in the *Beverley Guardian*, Thursday 20 July 1989) or at the eighteenth birthday party of their son Gary three years earlier (according to *Hull Daily Mail*, 27 July 1989). Although she moved out of the family home in Swinemoor Lane, Beverley she left her nine-year-old son David with her second husband. Whilst staying with Mrs Spinks, a fresh relationship developed between her and Alfred who lived in Bexley Heath, Kent. In early August 1988, they slept together for the first time in sixteen years. Alfred had taken her to the train station on the morning of Thursday, 4 August 1988, because David Simmonds had asked her if she wanted to return to the family home to see their son.

Part of Swinemoor Lane. The Author

On Friday, 5 August, police found Gillian Simmonds' naked body in the bath at the house in Swinemoor Lane. Four-and-a-half hours earlier, police had found her husband, unconscious, close to his car near Beverley. He had posted a suicide note to his sister, Mrs Joan Blanchard, asking her to bring up David and suggesting that she tell him they had died in a car crash. There were two cheques included in the letter: the one for Joan was for £16,900 and the other, for his solicitor, was for £450. After he had recovered, David Simmonds was charged with murder.

In July 1989, Simmonds appeared at York Crown Court. He admitted Gillian's manslaughter but the prosecution, led by David Barker QC would not accept his plea. Simmonds was a manager at ABI Caravans in Swinemoor Lane, and at the time of her death they were renting a house in the lane. Gillian had moved out a month before she was killed and had returned on the eve of their thirteenth wedding anniversary to see nine-year-old David. However, her husband had sent David to stay with his sister in Lincoln. Whilst she was there Simmonds had put sleeping pills into a mug of coffee. Gillian decided to have a bath before going on to Lincoln and, according to David, she had asked for a drink of whisky.

Pathologist, Dr Michael Green, who conducted a post-mortem

said that he found that there were bruises on her shoulder blades, elbow and neck. Her enlarged lungs had filled her chest cavity.

In his defence, Simmonds claimed that he had begged her to return but she had said she would not. She said she had loved her first husband throughout their marriage and that she had been living a lie. He described her as the 'best actress in the world'. She had taunted him about her affairs including one with her brother-in-law, Paul. She told him she had slept with Alfred the previous night and said she wanted him to hate her. He claimed there were taunts about her lovers being better than him and that he was 'a five minute wonder'. This drove him to push her head under the water. He had then left the house and tried to kill himself.

The seven men and five women jury took three and a half hours to unanimously find him guilty of murder – perhaps they took the view that sending David to Lincoln and drugging her indicated premeditation. Justice Donald Herrod QC said: 'This is a very sad day for you. Up to now you have led a blameless life and you did your best to be a good husband and you were a good father.' He then sentenced him to life, saying: 'You allowed your jealousy and emotions to get the better of you and you killed your wife so that no one else could have her.'

At the time he murdered Gillian, David Simmonds was also having an affair with a work colleague, one of a series he had had. A former neighbour said that 'if he said jump, Gillian would jump'. He would tell her to dress-up, even for a trip to the shops - yet he would go dressed casually.

2. Lincoln, 1999
Don't tell your husband

On Saturday, 29 May 1999, when Janet Richards, aged thirty-nine, failed to turn up for work at Lincoln's Usher Art Gallery her colleagues were concerned. They alerted the police and later that day her naked body was found on the bedroom floor at her home. A short time later the body of her lover was found in his fume-filled car on farmland two miles away.

Janet had recently been transferred from the Museum of Lincolnshire Life in Lincoln. Whilst she was there she meet a prisoner who worked there for three days a week as part of his pre-release programme. They had started an affair and Janet had moved out of the family home leaving her husband and the four children who lived there. She had not gone to live with her lover, she had moved into a house in Sincil Bank, Lincoln. Her lover was David Simmonds, aged fifty-three who had finally been released on licence the previous September.

Janet was aware that he was convicted of murdering his wife, it seems that he had told her his wife had had affairs with men who had called at the family home. One of the conditions of his day-release programme was that he did not have relationships with women, so their affair had to be kept from his probation officer. In mid-May Janet had decided to end their affair because Simmonds had become over possessive. Janet had become friendly with a plumber who had done some work for her, there was no relationship but it upset Simmonds. He implied that she was acting like his wife. She told him that their relationship was over – within days he had killed her. He found it hard to accept her rejection of him.

On Friday, 28 May, unemployed Simmonds had left his flat near Janet's and called on her. The meeting did not go well and he ended up strangling her – and then committing suicide. The police found a letter on her kitchen table. In it Simmonds begged her not to tell her husband or the authorities about their affair: 'We've been a secret for eighteen months. Now it's all over. Why don't you leave it like that? I'm begging you please.'

An inquest into both deaths was held over three days in December by Lincoln coroner Roger Atkinson. The inquest jury were told about Simmonds' conviction for murder and his release on licence from Morton Hall Prison. Friends of Janet's spoke about her affair with Simmonds. Emma Hammerton who worked at the museum had invited both of them for a meal at her home. They had got together after that evening but had to keep the affair quiet. Amanda Cooper said that Simmonds had told her about Janet and the plumber, and it had upset him. She had told Janet that he was upset and Janet said he had implied she was acting like his wife.

Lincolnshire Police stated that they had not been informed that a convicted murderer was released in their area by either the probation service or the prison service. On Wednesday, 15 December, the inquest jury returned verdicts of unlawful killing and suicide.

Chapter 20

Anthony McCullagh

Birmingham, 1989
Wakefield Prison, 1991

John Collins was the innocent victim of an unprovoked fatal stabbing by an enraged Anthony McCullagh in 1989. Given a life sentence, McCullagh – aware of his own mental health problems – with a fragile temper, killed again within two years of his imprisonment, at Wakefield. This time the source of his uncontrolled anger was triple-rapist, Kenneth Seaman.

1. Birmingham, 1989

I've stabbed a man...

John Collins, a nineteen-year-old metal worker, of Featherstone Road, Kings Heath, Birmingham had the misfortune to meet Anthony McCullagh in the street on Sunday, 2 July 1989. McCullagh forced John at knife-point into the playground of Colmore Road School in Kings Heath. John tried to appease him and even offered him his wallet but McCullagh was too angry with the world to be calmed down.

When McCullagh had seen John in the street he knew he would do him damage. When they got into the playground McCullagh stabbed him five times. John's calls for help resulted in him being taken to a nearby house and McCullagh called for an ambulance and told police officers that he had stabbed a man and thought he was dead. John Collins died in hospital three hours later. Following questioning, McCullagh was charged with the murder.

The case came to trial at Birmingham Crown Court on Monday, 10 November 1989. Although McCullagh pleaded guilty to murder, prosecuting counsel Mr Stuart Shields QC outlined the case. Anthony McCullagh was a twenty-two-year-old soldier based in Aldershot who was absent without leave from his unit, the Royal Transport Corps. On Saturday, 1 July 1989 he had been evicted from premises where he had lived. Filled with anger, on the Sunday he walked aimlessly around Birmingham and ended up in the Kings Heath area. It was there that he saw John Collins and decided to harm him. John had done nothing to provoke him and tried to calm the situation but McCullagh's anger with everyone needed an outlet. The five stab wounds that McCullagh inflicted seemed to bring him to his senses as he called for an ambulance. He had told the police that when he saw 'that boy' (John) in the street he just had to do him harm. He hated everything and could give no reason for the attack except that he felt uncontrollable anger.

McCullagh's defence counsel, Mr Anthony Palmer QC said that he had asked his client if he had anything to say to which he had replied that he was sorry. The house eviction probably caused feelings of rejection, so without friends and colleagues he felt there was no future and in this depressed state he hated everything. He came upon John whilst in this condition and John died as a result of being in the wrong place at the wrong time.

Justice Hodgson sentenced McCullagh to life. Less than two years later he was to kill again, this time in a Yorkshire prison.

2. Wakefield Prison, 1991

He wasn't a 'nonce'

On Friday, 19 July 1991, a small report appeared on the front page of the *Wakefield Express*. It said that police had started a murder investigation at Wakefield Prison following the fatal stabbing of Kenneth Seaman, of Southfield Road, Middlesbrough, a thirty-seven-year-old rapist serving a life sentence. He had been found dying in his cell in C Wing at twenty-past four on the afternoon of Wednesday, 17 July. A twenty-four-year-old prisoner was being questioned. That was the only report in the *Wakefield Express*, there was no report about anyone being charged with his murder.

In July 1992, Anthony McCullagh, aged twenty-five, originally from Chester-le-Street, stood trial at Durham Crown Court on the charge of murdering Kenneth Seaman. McCullagh denied the charge, saying he had not intended to kill him. He had gone into Seaman's cell to confront him, as the latter (a convicted triple-rapist) had supposedly called him a 'nonce' which is slang for a sex offender.

Sometime before he went to Kenneth's cell, McCullagh made a knife from a sliver of mirror glass. He attacked Seaman with it and then left. When he was found, Kenneth Seaman was still alive but died before an ambulance arrived. Counsel for McCullagh, Roger Keen QC said that McCullagh suffered from an inherited personality disorder, which caused him difficulty in controlling his

The formidable walls of Wakefield Prison. The Author

temper on some occasions. He was aware of his problem and whilst in prison he had on three occasions insisted on seeing the prison doctor and psychiatrist as he felt he would harm someone if he was not admitted to the prison hospital. His client wanted help with his problem before he was released from prison; he would give his full co-operation to the prison service or other authorities.

On Friday, 10 July it took the jury two and a half hours to reach their unanimous verdict of guilty to the murder charge. Mr Justice Waite imposed the only sentence possible: life imprisonment. He said he would pass on psychiatrists' reports and a letter from McCullagh in which he asks for help with his problem, to the authorities.

Chapter 21

Christopher Anness
(aka Kenneth Valentine)

Leeds, 1990
Bradford, 1996

In 1991 Christopher Anness – who had previous convictions involving sexual assault and robbery – was found guilty (of manslaughter) for the death of Janet Willoughby. Following extreme sexual activity, Anness tried to hide her body in a cupboard.

For this he was given a seven-year custodial sentence. Five years later, Annes – or Valentine as he became legally known – killed again. His victim was a twenty-five-year-old prostitute who was assaulted, strangled and placed in a culvert. His life sentence included a recommended twenty-two year minimum term prior to any parole consideration.

1. Leeds, 1990

He blamed her boyfriend

There are occasional reports about bodies being found in homes months or years after the person died and no one had noticed the person was no longer around. Janet Willoughby's disappearance was soon noticed. A friend was concerned when she had not seen her on Wednesday, 16 May 1990 so contacted the police. The friend's concern was such that the police forced their way into Janet's flat, at Holburn Towers, Woodhouse, Leeds that same evening. Janet, a Leeds United fan, was twenty-one-years-old and unemployed. She lived in the ground floor flat by herself. A search resulted in her body

Holborn Towers, Woodhouse, Leeds. D Speight

being found in a cupboard.

As is usual in most homicide cases, the police looked into those closest to her and took her boyfriend, Richard Bonass, in for questioning. He told the police that he, Janet and a friend, Kenneth Christopher Anness had been playing Scrabble into the early hours of the morning. When he had left to go to work, Kenneth Anness was still in the flat. The police then brought Anness in for questioning. After further enquiries, Richard Bonass was released and Anness, of Oatlands Heights, Little London, Leeds, was charged with the murder of Janet Willoughby.

In March 1991, the case came to trial at Leeds Crown Court. The prosecution case was presented by Martin Bethel QC and Anness was defended by Franz Muller QC. The Crown's case was that thirty-six-year-old Anness killed Janet when she spurned his sexual advances; she had been tied to the bed and whipped. Janet had died of internal injuries following a sexual assault. During the cross-examination of Janet's boyfriend, Franz Muller sought to implicate him in her death. He suggested that Janet had died as a result of sexual activity that had gone wrong and that he had put her body in the cupboard. Richard Bonass denied any involvement in her death.

In his defence, Anness said that Janet was alive when he left her flat. On Monday, 25 March, after five hours of deliberations the jury acquitted Anness of murder but convicted him of manslaughter. Mr Justice May said that anybody would shrink with horror from the consequences of what he had done but the jury had acquitted him of murder, so he took it that the jury decided that Anness had not intended to cause really serious bodily harm. The judge commented on Anness' previous convictions which included indecent assault, one of which involved a young girl; and he had also been sentenced to seven years for robbery in January 1985, but released in July 1989.

In mitigation, Franz Muller said that Anness himself had been subject to a sexual assault when he was young. His previous offences were wholly different to the manslaughter conviction. Muller claimed that the evidence clearly showed that there was an element of consent from Janet. However, Justice May said: 'I accept these offences were some time ago and they do not match together with the one you have been convicted on but I cannot ignore that there are sexual offences in your background.' He then sentenced Anness to seven years, the same length of sentence he had received for the robbery.

2. Bradford, 1996

It wasn't his rug

Michelle Routledge, also known as 'Blondie', was concerned for her friend Caroline Creevy's welfare. She had not seen her since Monday 28 October 1996. On 1 November, she reported her disappearance to the police. Michelle had met Caroline when they were both working as prostitutes in Bradford. On the Monday morning they were working in the Thornton Road area when a client had taken both of them to his home. Afterwards, he had driven them so they could buy drugs, then he dropped Caroline off in Thornton Road. That was the last time Michelle had seen her.

Caroline Creevy, aged twenty-five, had been living in the flat of a man called Kenneth Valentine, in Soho Mills, Thornton Road. Caroline and Michelle knew that he had served time for killing a man. Caroline paid him £5 for each client she took back to the flat.

Thornton Road, Bradford. D Speight

When Michelle had reported Caroline's disappearance she told the police that on the evening of Tuesday 29 October she had gone to Soho Mills to see Caroline. She used the intercom to call the flat and over it she heard a female voice screaming: 'Help me!' After a while, another of the flat's residents let her in and she went up to the top floor flat. Michelle got no reply to her knocking on the door so she looked through the letter box but could not see anything as the room was in darkness. After waiting a while, she left but returned later that evening. On that occasion it was clear that Valentine was in and she noticed that the furniture had been rearranged and a rug was missing. He said he had got rid of it because he had spilled paint on it. When the police heard what Michelle had to say they were also concerned. A prostitute going missing for a few days does not usually warrant a police investigation but Kenneth Valentine had not yet changed his name by deed poll from Kenneth Anness. Under his real name he was known to the West Yorkshire police because of his 1991 manslaughter conviction for the manslaughter of Janet Willoughby in Leeds.

As part of their investigation the police looked at security videos of Soho Mills. On one, a man was seen carrying an object under his arm down the rear staircase at ten-past one on the morning of Wednesday 30 October. Later on, a man was seen leaving the flats by the rear fire exit, carrying a large object over his shoulder; and was seen returning twenty-three minutes later. When questioned about Caroline's disappearance, 'Valentine' said that he had last seen her on the Monday night when she was with two black men. He said she had taken some clothes with her and a front door key to his flat.

On 17 November 1996, a police underwater team found Caroline's body in a culvert under Goit Side, Bradford. Her body had been wrapped in a rug which had black plastic bags encasing it. The police then took 'Anness' in for further questioning, who had now changed his name to Kenneth Valentine. The post-mortem revealed that Caroline had died as a result of strangulation. She also had a broken nose, bruises to both arms and there were eight bruises on her face and head. She had been dressed in only a black skirt when she was placed in the rug. On

Goit Side, Bradford. D Speight

Thursday 21 November, forty-two-year-old Kenneth Valentine appeared before Bradford magistrates charged with Caroline's murder.

Valentine appeared for trial at Leeds Crown Court in March 1998. The prosecution case was outlined by Anton Lodge QC. Caroline left her home in Huddersfield soon after she was sixteen. For most of the time she worked as a prostitute in Huddersfield and Bradford. When working in the Bradford area in 1996, Caroline and Michelle had paid a man (not Valentine) £5 per client to use his flat in Soho Mills. Caroline's boyfriend was arrested so she went to Huddersfield to stay with a friend. She returned to Bradford a week later and stayed at Valentine's flat. As she was bringing her clients to his flat she started to pay him £5 each time, too.

Caroline's friend, Michelle, told the jury about the evening of 29 October – how she 'buzzed' Valentine's flat and heard a woman's voice screaming: 'Help me!' and how she gained entry to the flats when another resident of the flats opened the door. Going up to Valentine's top-floor flat and knocking on the door but getting no

The culvert where Caroline's body was found. D Speight

reply. Looking through the letterbox into the flat's hallway and finding it in darkness. How she waited outside his door for a while but hearing no sound she eventually left. She told them that she returned later that evening and saw Valentine in his flat, he explained the missing rug to her by saying he had spilled paint on it. He told Michelle he had not seen Caroline since the Monday night when she was in the company of two men.

Detective Constable Neil Parry gave evidence concerning Valentine's police interviews. He had denied murdering Caroline, he said that he was not the man in the security videos seen carrying something out of the building in the early hours of the morning of the 30 October. He had admitted that he allowed Caroline to bring her clients back to the flat and she had been living in the flat prior to her death. When he was shown a photograph of the rug that had been used to enclose Caroline's body, he denied it was the one from his flat. He said that witnesses who said it was his were wrong. The one he threw away was similar to the one in the photo but not the same. He also denied that he had ever been to the culvert where she was found.

On Thursday, 26 March 1998, the seven-woman and five-man jury, unanimously found him guilty of murdering Caroline Creevy. They were then told about his previous conviction for manslaughter. When sentencing him to life, Justice Ognall, made a recommendation that he serve twenty-two years before being considered for release on parole. He commented that Anness'/Valentine's record and the evidence presented in this case abundantly demonstrate that he was a very dangerous man.

Chapter 22

David Sandham

Fleetwood, 1996
Cornholme (Todmorden), 2002

D avid Sandham fatally stabbed his brother during a domestic incident in 1996. Found guilty of manslaughter, he was given a five-year custodial sentence. Six years later, in a most unusual case involving witchcraft, Sandham and his friend, Daniel Delker were found guilty of the brutal murder of James Bowman.

1. Fleetwood, 1996

He's stabbed me,
get an ambulance

David Terence Sandham, aged seventeen, and a few of his friends, had been drinking at his home in London Street, Fleetwood, Lancashire, on Friday, 12 April 1996. In the afternoon, David's nineteen-year-old unemployed elder brother Tony, returned home and found the house to be in a mess. He told David to wash up before their father returned. David said he would do it after he had been out. Tony and David argued and Tony punched and kicked David who then started to do the washing up. Whilst he was doing this he picked up a knife to clean it and, as Tony talked on the phone, stabbed him in the chest, leaving the knife embedded there. An ambulance was called. When the paramedics arrived they found Tony on the floor with the knife plunged in his chest virtually up to the hilt. Tony died at the scene. After the stabbing, David had run

Sketch of David Sandham. Carl Lawson

out of the house. An hour later he went to Fleetwood Police Station and told Alan Barnes, a civilian worker at the reception desk, that he had stabbed his brother. A police officer was called and David Sandham was then arrested, questioned and charged with murder. He was allowed out on bail, to live at Ormerod Street, Thornton Cleveleys.

The case was heard at Preston Crown Court in March 1997 with Justice Forbes presiding. As David Sandham was under eighteen his name could not be disclosed by the press. The Crown's case was presented by Tim Holroyde and David Sandham was defended by Eric Somerset-Jones QC. David was prepared to plead guilty to manslaughter but the Crown wanted him tried for murder. The cause of death was a single stab wound to the heart and a pathologist, Dr Edmund Tapp, said that considerable force would have been needed as the knife had gone through the heart, part of the left lung and struck a rib in the deceased's back. David said that his brother had physically and verbally abused him for years and that whilst he was washing up he was feeling humiliated and thinking of all the times he had been beaten by him. Tony Sandham was his brother but not his friend. His mind had gone blank when he stabbed him and the next thing he remembered was standing in the doorway and Tony was staring at him. Tony had then said: 'He's stabbed me, get an ambulance.' When Tony had bent over with his hands holding the knife in his chest David had run out. David now had difficulty sleeping and had nightmares about the stabbing.

On Thursday, 6 March 1997, after a four-day trial, the jury, comprised of seven men and six women, took four hours to reach their verdict. They convicted David Sandham of manslaughter on the grounds of provocation. Justice Forbes said: 'This is a very sad and tragic case. You are responsible for the death of your own brother. You had a sudden and temporary loss of self control as a result of his physical and verbal bullying. There is a long history of it and you suffered much. However, the crime you have committed is very serious indeed, so serious only a custodial sentence is justified.' He then sentenced David Sandham to five years. The ban on reporting his name was lifted following his conviction.

2. Cornholme, 2002
He definitely had Melanie under a spell

Witchcraft seldom features in modern murder cases but it did in this unusual case. Dean Crowther was walking with his young son and their dogs on Sunday, 15 September 2002 – on the hillside near Cornholme, West Yorkshire. Near to a rock formation called Back Wood he saw what appeared to be clothing about thirty yards away but he was dubious so he took his son to a nearby relative's house in Burnley Road. He borrowed a mobile phone and returned to the scene, where he found a badly injured man. The man died before an ambulance and police arrived. It was clear that the deceased had suffered many injuries and Detective Superintendent Allan Doherty set up a murder inquiry and arrests were soon made.

A witness said that she had heard shouting on the hillside at eight that morning. A search of the man's clothing had revealed a prescription with an address in nearby Ernest Street. Police soon sealed off the terraced house and arrested the occupiers: Melanie Payne, aged forty-four and her twenty-one-year-old son Nicholas Grundy.

The hillside at Cornholme, accessed via footpath and this road. The Author

The victim was identified as Melanie's ex-lover, James Bowman, an unemployed forty-four-year old drifter who was camping on the hillside having been told to leave her home on the Friday. On Monday, the police arrested Melanie's other son, Daniel Antonious Delker, aged twenty-three of Preston, Lancashire, and his friend, David Terance Sandham, also aged twenty-three of Cleveley, Blackpool. On Friday the two of them were charged with his murder and Melanie and Nicholas had earlier been released on police bail. On Saturday, Nicholas was also charged with the murder and remanded in custody. The next day, nine police officers questioned 280 people in the Burnley Road/ Ernest Street area between seven and ten-thirty the previous morning. The Calder Valley Search and Rescue Team searched a 100m by 200m area of steep banking in an effort to find clues or weapons.

Efforts were made to trace the deceased's family. Bowman was born Vincent Alfred James Fayer on 26 April 1958 in Liverpool and had changed his name to James Bowman. His funeral service was held at Park Wood Crematorium, Elland on Thursday, 27 March.

The case came to trial at Leeds Crown Court on 30 April 2003 with Justice Gage presiding and David Hatton QC prosecuting. The jury consisted of six men and six women. James, who had an interest in witchcraft, had met Melanie at a psychic fair in Todmorden in the spring of 2002. Melanie was interested in the earth religion 'Shambala' and was living in Todmorden at the time. Shortly afterwards, she moved to Cornholme and James moved in with her and her son.

The prosecution case was that Melanie had phoned her son, Daniel Delker, on Friday, 13 September, asking him to come as she had asked Bowman to leave that day and was worried that he might harass her. Daniel decided to take his friend, David Sandham, along and they arrived at five pm on the Saturday. On the Friday night Nicholas had seen a lamp shining on the hillside and in the morning wild flowers had been found left outside. On the Sunday morning a witness had seen the three of them going up the hillside. The Crown claimed this was to warn James off but for some unknown reason the warning became a violent attack

Janesse Mousea, a friend of Melanie's, said of James: 'He was into Wiccan witchcraft. I did not ever want to learn that stuff. It uses imagery of sex. I did not like his whole sense of presence.' Grundy's (Melanie's son) counsel Douglas Hogg QC, said to her: 'He engaged in a form of witchcraft that you found very unsavoury, it relies in part on sexual domination and Mr Bowman made himself the dominant partner in any sexual relationship.' Ms Mousea's reply was: 'He definitely had Melanie under a spell.' She said that Grundy did not like James and he had told people that he wanted to kill him but she thought he did not mean it. 'He was a bit protective but he was a very good son.'

Delker's girlfriend, Rebecca McCracken, told the court that Delker and Sandham had gone to his mother's that Saturday because she was having trouble with her former boyfriend. When they returned on the Sunday she had washed their soiled trousers. She had also overheard part of a conversation they had, which included the words 'hillside', 'a camp fire' and 'hitting and kicking' but she told them she did not want to hear anymore. Cross-examined by Delker's counsel, Paul Reid, QC, she said that she had not mentioned the conversation to the police straight away because she had forgotten about it but she denied it was a conversation months before the incident. Miss Sarah Gilbert, Sandham's partner, also gave evidence about the conversation she had overheard.

Dr Deborah Sharp, a forensic scientist, reported that she had found blood mixed with mud on Delker's boots after his arrest. DNA testing showed a billion to one chance that it came from someone unrelated to James Bowman. Blood found on Sandham's trainers also matched the profile, indicating that the wearer had been in close or direct contact with James's wet blood.

Professor Christopher Milroy reported that James had died from the effects of stab wounds and head injuries. The two most serious stab wounds were to his back, they had penetrated to his chest. There were at least twenty head injuries caused by a rock or similar weapon, the one above his right eye had caused a fracture and brain damage. There were more than eighty-eight injures in total. James could have taken two hours to die from his injuries and Prof Milroy agreed that the stab wounds could have occurred after the head injuries. He had a broken finger that could have been caused when he was being battered but he had no injuries indicating that he had attempted to defend himself against a knife. Dr Carl Gray, who was present during a second post-mortem gave his opinion that linear wounds on James's head could have been caused by the shaft of a golf club. He said the head injuries were more likely to have been caused before the stab wounds.

Miss Elizabeth Bottomley was walking her dog on the morning of the murder and had seen a man with a golf club in the area of the killing. A statement was read out, and in it Frederick Foster-Brayshaw said that on that morning he had heard shouting coming from the wood, sounding like a man and a woman arguing. Ms Mary-Ellen Moccia said she saw a man and a woman around the same time and they were acting suspicious.

Detective Constable Nicholas Clay said that in an interview Delker had said he had gone to see his mother on the weekend with his friend, Sandham. He had heard of James through his mother and thought he was homeless and another one of the 'charity case-types' his mother liked to help. His mother told him James had left wild flowers on the wall that morning and she thought they were to do with a voodoo spell but he did not believe in such 'claptrap'. That evening he went walking with Sandham and they got mud on their trousers in a bog so they had borrowed some of his brother's trousers to travel back to Lancashire.

In a police interview, Nicholas Grundy said that he was concerned about his mother's relationship with James and his interest in witchcraft. After his mother had started a relationship with James she was hospitalised for a month suffering from a breakdown. During the breakdown she had acted in a sexual manner towards him, friends and hospital staff. When she left hospital she went with James to Glastonbury and the New Forest. Back in Cornholme, she became depressed and James appeared to resent looking after her. James had claimed to have been in the SAS. Grundy could not remember if that weekend he had walked on the hillside where James was found. On Thursday, 8 May, Grundy was acquitted of the murder on the direction of Justice Gage who said there was insufficient evidence against him.

In court Delker claimed that the blood on his boot was because he had accidentally kicked James in the face. He had got up in the middle of the Saturday night to let out one of his mother's dogs.

When he did this he saw someone near the house making gestures with his hand over a bunch of flowers. He ran up to them and threw a punch but the man backed away so Delker put his hands on the wall and swung his feet over – and that was when his boot made contact with James. The man asked if he was in trouble, then left saying he was going to the coast, and Delker returned to the house. When asked by his counsel, John Bromley-Davenport: 'In particular you were not involved in the attack on him on the hillside that led to his death?' Delker replied: 'No.'

Sketch of James Bowman. Carl Lawson

David Sandham said that he had never met James, and that he had stayed the night in Ernest Street. The following morning he had gone for a walk with Delker and Nicholas. He had smoked cannabis on the walk on the nearby hills but he had not seen James. During the walk he had fallen into a bog and got his jeans and trainers muddy so he had changed them. When he got to Delker's home in Lancashire they had both washed their jeans. He was not aware that James' blood was on his trainers and he could not explain how it had got there. Dr Sharp denied that the blood could have been transferred from Delker's boots. The jury were informed that a friend of Sandham and Delker, Steven Beacher, had been asked to accompany them to Cornholme that weekend for the sole purpose of dealing with James.

On Thursday, 15 May the jury found them both guilty of murder by a ten to two majority verdict. After the trial, Detective Superintendent Allan Doherty said of James Bowman: 'We did not find any terrible record of domestic violence which would warrant an attack on him of this kind. He did not deserve to die.' He had been sentenced to three years in 1973 for rape. Then in 1985 he had been jailed for six years for indecent assault, robbery and abduction. These convictions had been years ago and he had seemed to have got on with his life until his murder.

Chapter 23

Stephen Crowther

Leeds, 1997 and 2000

Stephen Crowther killed his brother in a fit of jealousy in 1997 and was convicted of manslaughter. A knife was the weapon used. Three years later, he killed again. On this occasion the victim was his girlfriend, stabbed with a kitchen knife.

1. Beeston, Leeds, 1997

His brother was keen on his girlfriend...

Stephen Crowther's first conviction was on 24 February 1998, when he pleaded guilty to manslaughter. He had stabbed his elder brother Andrew in the back of his knee during an argument. He had realised that Andrew was also keen on his girlfriend. The three of them had shared a bedsit but Crowther and his girlfriend had moved into a flat in Cranbrook Avenue, Beeston, Leeds. He told her not to let Andrew into their place but he would visit when he was at work.

One afternoon in July 1997, Andrew and the girl had been drinking. Later that night he called at the flat but Crowther would not let him in. Andrew then said that he wanted his stereo back. Crowther then gave the stereo to his girlfriend so that she could go down and give it him. When she opened the door, Andrew rushed past her and into the flat. Crowther told Andrew to leave but he wouldn't, so the argument got worse and Crowther stabbed Andrew in the back of the knee. Unfortunately, the knife cut an artery in his leg which resulted in massive blood loss and unconsciousness.

Following Andrew's death, Stephen Crowther, then aged twenty, was charged with his brother's murder. The murder charged was dropped when he pleaded guilty to manslaughter. Prosecuting counsel was James Spencer QC and Crowther was defended by Geoffrey Marson QC. Mr Marson said that Crowther had not intended to seriously harm Andrew. They were generally close but occasionally fought like cat and dog.

Justice Ognall sentenced Crowther to four years imprisonment. He said it was clear that Andrew was largely to blame for what happened. Crowther had tried to avoid the problem by not letting him in but Andrew had pushed his way in and 'caused the trouble'.

2. Beeston, Leeds, 2000
Don't let her die!

Anthony Newlands heard the frantic knocking on his door on the night of Monday, 18 December 2000. Opening it, he saw a man he recognised from the bedsit opposite (Stephen Crowther), and he had blood on him. The man said his girlfriend was bleeding to death and asked if Anthony knew any first aid. Anthony said he did so they ran to the bedsit, where he found a girl unconscious on the sofa. She had a wound to her left shoulder. The girl was bleeding and breathing heavily but her pulse was normal. Whilst Anthony did what he could, the man kept shouting: 'Don't let her die!'

The ambulance and police soon arrived at Linden Avenue, Beeston, Leeds and she was rushed to Leeds General Infirmary.

Linden Road, Beeston. D. Speight

Thornton Lollies, Morley. The Author

Doctors struggled for hours to stop the bleeding but she died four hours after admission. Her parents in Bradford had been informed of her injury and they were there before she died.

The man who raised the alarm was questioned by the police. His version of events was that he had woken to find his sixteen-year-old girlfriend, Nicola Garena, bleeding on the sofa. The police were very sceptical about his version of events, as twenty-four-year-old Stephen Crowther was known to West Yorkshire Police. In February 1998, he had been convicted of manslaughter at Leeds Crown Court. After further enquiries Crowther was charged with murdering Nicola Garena. The trial took place at Leeds Crown Court in November 2001. The Crown's case was presented by Andrew Robertson QC. He said that on the fateful evening the couple had drunk a bottle of vodka, four tins of lager and had smoked cannabis in their flat. Nicola had met Crowther when she got a temporary job at Thornton Lollies, Ackroyd Street, Morley. At the time he was a forklift truck driver but after a while he became a trainee manager. They were soon living together at an uncle's of his in Beeston. On 15 December 2000, they moved into the bedsit in Linden Road. Evidence was heard from neighbours who said they heard a woman screaming: 'Get off me, get off me you bastard.'

Christopher Milroy, an Home Office pathologist, said that the stab wound had cut an important vein and caused one of her lungs to collapse. She had been stabbed with a kitchen knife.

A statement made by Crowther to the police was read out to the court. In it he claimed that at least one of them had dozed off, Nicola on the sofa and himself on the chair. He had woken to a gargling sound made by Nicola. Looking over to her he had seen blood on her top. He had removed her fleece and T-shirt to see what was causing the bleeding then he had gone to a neighbour for help. In an interview, Crowther claimed he had never laid a finger on Nicola and he did not know how she had been stabbed. He claimed that they had always got on really well and were due to get engaged. As there was no signs of a forced entry to the bedsit and neighbours had heard an argument between the couple, the jury did not believe his account of the events. What caused the argument is only known to Crowther. On Thursday 8 November the jury took less than two hours to return with a guilty verdict on the murder charge.

Justice Maurice Kay then sentenced him to life. He said to Crowther: 'Within the space of three and a half years you killed your brother and now your girlfriend. You must be a very dangerous young man when you have drink and when you lose your temper and there is a knife nearby. It will be a very long time before anyone gives serious consideration to your release.'

After the trial, Nicola's mother, Katrina, said that Nicola had been devastated when her father died when she was ten years old. She had never seen Crowther but had spoken to him on the phone. She did not believe his claim that they were going to get engaged as Nicola was planning to come home at Christmas in order to get away from him. Katrina thought that Nicola had no plans to return to Crowther.

Chapter 24

James Paton

Leeds, 1998
Bradford, 2005

James Paton was convicted of manslaughter in 1998 after a fatal attack on a fifty-seven-year-old man following an argument. Seven years later and only two years after being released from prison Paton killed again.

1. Leeds, 1998

He had not intended to kill...

On Monday, 12 October 1999, eighteen-year-old James Paton had denied a murder charge at Leeds Crown Court. His plea of guilty to manslaughter, however, was accepted.

Prosecutor James Stewart QC outlined the case to the court. Paton lived in Recreation Terrace, Holbeck. On Saturday, 19 September 1998, he had gone to his aunt's home in Francis Street, Chapeltown. Theodore Walters, a fifty-seven-year-old former foundry worker lived opposite his aunt and was also visiting when Paton was there. An argument developed when Theodore drank some of Jean's (Paton's aunt's) brandy. He said he would go and get a bottle of vodka but he needed to go to the bathroom first. Paton had then gone to the bathroom and he was angered by the state Theodore had left it in. He punched Theodore who fell backwards into the bath, then he kicked him twice in the stomach. The force of the blows meant that Theodore's head struck the bath each time. Theodore must have then returned home, as a report in the *Halifax Evening Courier* dated Thursday, 8 October 1998, stated that he had been found in his home on 19 September. It also said that an

Francis Street, Leeds. D Speight

eighteen-year-old had been charged with his murder following Theodore's death on 5 October.

Paton, on seeing an ambulance taking Theodore to hospital, had used the keys he had found in the bathroom to gain entry to Theodore's home, where he then stole a video recorder. Theodore had suffered three broken ribs and tears to his bowel, liver and duodenum. His condition appeared to be improving but a blood clot caused his death. Paton's counsel, Peter Wright, said that his client was only eighteen at the time and had not meant to seriously harm Theodore.

Justice Brian Walsh QC, the Recorder of Leeds, sentenced Paton to six and a half years in a young offenders' institution. He accepted that he had not intended to seriously injure Theodore. But he also commented: 'If ever there was a cowardly and despicable act of burglary that was it.'

New Lane, Laisterdyke. D Speight

Paton's aunt, Jean Cairns, was cleared of assisting Paton after the offence. She had also been charged with 'handling' two of Theodore's rings, but that charge was ordered to lie on file.

2. Bradford, 2005

They were not at the hostel

Chris (Christopher) Ruane was preparing lunch at his home in New Lane, Laisterdyke, Bradford on Tuesday, 12 July 2005. As he was getting it ready his wife Diane was upstairs. At half-past two there was a knock at the back door and Chris opened it. Two men then rushed in. One of them attacked Chris with a knife and the other punched him. Hearing the disturbance, Diane came down the stairs and saw Chris being attacked. She shouted at the men to stop but it had no effect. Diane then jumped on the knifeman's back in an attempt to protect Chris. The knifeman responded by stabbing Diane in the neck and body. As badly injured Chris and Diane struggled to the front door to raise the alarm, the two men stole some items and fled.

James Davey heard Chris Ruane shouting: 'Help, Jimmy help, we've been stabbed!' as they struggled down their drive. Diane had a throat wound and was soon slumped on the pavement. James Davey rushed to call for an ambulance before he returned to them. Chris and Diane were rushed to Bradford Royal Infirmary where Diane died an hour later.

Detective Superintendent Paul Kennedy was put in charge of the murder investigation. Searching the house and surrounding area led to the discovery that Diane's handbag and purse were missing, as was a set of ornamental knives. A bloodstained knife was then found in a garden near to their home.

Although fifty-eight-year-old scrap metal dealer Chris Ruane was seriously injured and was to spend three days in hospital, he was soon telling DS Kennedy that he knew one of the attackers. James Paton aged twenty-five was a former neighbour and had visited them on several occasions, to sell some goods. He had called at the house earlier that day but had left following an argument.

James Paton was not at the Salvation Army hostel in Leeds Road, Bradford when they called to see him. Another hostel resident was missing: Carl Brady, aged twenty-eight, who was being supervised by the probation service through Community Orders, for theft. At the time they were both on bail. Within a week both of them had been arrested in Scarborough. They were brought back to Bradford and charged with the murder of Diane Ruane and wounding Chris Ruane, with intent.

On Monday, 7 March 2006, James Paton and Carl Brady appeared at Bradford Crown Court for the start of the trial. The hearing was soon adjourned and after several hours they reappeared in the dock and pleaded guilty to both the murder and wounding charges. Justice Stephen Gullick said he would sentence them the next day.

On the Tuesday, Paton's counsel said that the attack was not premeditated or motivated by the desire to murder or rob. Brady's counsel, Alistair MacDonald, said his client accepted that he was a joint partner in the assaults but he had not used a knife nor had he inflicted the fatal wounds. After the case, DS Kennedy, said that the attack actually was premeditated, vicious and frenzied. Justice Gullick sentenced Brady to twenty years and thirty-nine days with a concurrent eight years for the wounding offence. Brady had fifteen previous convictions including, theft, robbery and dishonesty.

Paton was sentenced to twenty-four years and 139 days. He had eighteen previous convictions, including the manslaughter case referred to earlier.

James Paton had been released from prison in November 2003 having served four years of the six-and-a-half-year sentence for that offence.

On Wednesday, 28 June 2006, the Appeal Court ruled that Paton and Brady could challenge the terms of their sentences. Justice Cox said: 'There are arguable issuses relating to the terms specified in each case.'

On Thursday, 26 October 2006, the Court of Appeal reduced Paton's tariff by two years and Brady's by four years.

TRUE CRIME FROM WHARNCLIFFE

Foul Deeds and Suspicious Deaths Series

Barking, Dagenham & Chadwell Heath
Barnsley
Bath
Bedford
Birmingham
Black Country
Blackburn and Hyndburn
Bolton
Bradford
Brighton
Bristol
Cambridge
Carlisle
Chesterfield
Colchester
Coventry
Croydon
Derby
Durham
Ealing
Folkestone and Dover
Grimsby
Guernsey
Guildford
Halifax
Hampstead, Holborn and St Pancras
Huddersfield
Hull

Leeds
Leicester
Lewisham and Deptford
Liverpool
London's East End
London's West End
Manchester
Mansfield
More Foul Deeds Birmingham
More Foul Deeds Chesterfield
More Foul Deeds Wakefield
Newcastle
Newport
Norfolk
Northampton
Nottingham
Oxfordshire
Pontefract and Castleford
Portsmouth
Rotherham
Scunthorpe
Southend-on-Sea
Staffordshire and the Potteries
Stratford and South Warwickshire
Tees
Warwickshire
Wigan
York

OTHER TRUE CRIME BOOKS FROM WHARNCLIFFE

A-Z Yorkshire Murder
Black Barnsley
Brighton Crime and Vice 1800-2000
Durham Executions
Essex Murders
Executions & Hangings in Newcastle
    and Morpeth
Norfolk Mayhem and Murder

Norwich Murders
Strangeways Hanged
The A-Z of London Murders
Unsolved Murders in Victorian and
    Edwardian London
Unsolved Norfolk Murders
Unsolved Yorkshire Murders
Yorkshire's Murderous Women

Please contact us via any of the methods below for more information
or a catalogue.

WHARNCLIFFE BOOKS

47 Church Street – Barnsley – South Yorkshire – S70 2AS
Tel: 01226 734555 – 734222 Fax: 01226 – 734438
E-mail: enquiries@pen-and-sword.co.uk
Website: www.wharncliffebooks.co.uk

Index